PILATES & YOGA

PILATES & YOGA

JUDY SMITH • EMILY KELLY • JONATHAN MONKS

METRO BOOKS
NEW YORK

© Anness Publishing Ltd 2004, 2007

This 2006 edition published by Metro Books,
by arrangement with Anness Publishing Ltd

Publisher: Joanna Lorenz

Project Editors: Katy Bevan, Debra Mayhew and Catherine Stuart

Production Controller: Don Campaniello

Editorial Readers: Lindsay Zamponi and Jay Thundercliffe

New Material: Kim Davies provided the text for
pages 6 to 7 and 10 to 13.

Iyengar Yoga | pages 8 to 45

Author: Judy Smith

Consultant: Jeanne Maslen

Designer: Anita Schnable and Ann Samuel

Photography: Clare Park, with additional photography by Bonieventure Bagalue.

Pilates | pages 46 to 131

Author: Emily Kelly

Designer: Lisa Tai

Photography: Christine Hanscomb (colour); Stephen Swain (black-and-white).

Illustrator: David Cook, Linden Artists

Photography: John Freeman, assisted by Alex Dow

Models: Carly Milnes and Lesley Portner.

Yoga-Pilates | pages132 to 251

Author: Jonathan Monks

Designer: Adelle Morris

Metro Books

122 Fifth Avenue

New York, NY 10011

ISBN-13: 978-0-7607- 8001 5

ISBN-10: 0-7607-8001-3

Printed and bound in China

1 0 9 8 7 6 5 4 3

Previously published in three separate volumes as *Iyengar Yoga, Emily Kelly's Commonsense Pilates* and *Yoga-Pilates*

Disclaimer

The author and publishers have made every effort to ensure that all instructions contained within this book are accurate and safe, and cannot accept liability for any resulting injury, damage or loss to persons or property, however it may arise. If you do have any special needs or problems, consult your doctor or a physiotherapist. This book cannot replace medical consultation and should be used in conjunction with professional advice.

Previously published in three separate volumes as *Iyengar Yoga, Emily Kelly's Commonsense Pilates* and *Yoga-Pilates*

Contents

Holistic Fitness: Exercising Mind and Body

More and more of us are looking for fitness programmes that address not just the body but the mind, too. We are turning to holistic forms of exercise that aim to develop the whole person. Yoga and Pilates are the two leading forms of mind-body fitness taught in the West. Practised regularly, they can benefit every aspect of our lives, from our posture to our moods, and our physical well-being to our sense of happiness and peace.

Yoga and Pilates have evolved as they have been taught and studied, and as our understanding of the body has developed. They continue to be refined as people seek new ways of maintaining their well-being despite busy lifestyles. Yoga-Pilates is the latest incarnation of mind-body exercise: a practice that draws on both systems to create a dynamic and fully integrated workout.

This book aims to give you everything you need to establish a holistic exercise programme for yourself. There are separate sections on yoga and Pilates, written by respected practitioners in the field. Each can be used to help you develop and deepen your understanding of the practice. The final section, Yoga-Pilates, shows how to combine the two disciplines into one complete workout for your mind and body.

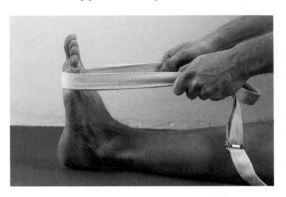

above Yoga is infinitely flexible. You can adapt the postures to suit your needs and limitations, and use props such as belts to help you achieve and maintain a pose.

What is yoga?

Yoga is the best possible exercise there is for improving suppleness. However, yoga postures are more than physical poses; they work on the mind and spirit, and promote increased awareness, vitality and inner peace.

There are many forms of yoga: astanga, for example, is flowing and dynamic, while Shivananda is very gentle. Iyengar yoga, covered in the first section of this book, is the most precise method. It was developed in the 1960s by an advanced practitioner B.K.S. Iyengar, who wanted to integrate modern thinking about the body with the ancient system he had studied for many years.

Iyengar emphasizes the importance of correct alignment at all times. All the poses can be modified, depending on the student's abilities and flexibility. Equipment, such as blocks and straps, is used to help practitioners get into postures without straining joints or overstretching muscles. This attention to detail makes Iyengar yoga very safe, provided that it is practised with care and with respect to the body's limitations.

What is Pilates?

Pilates is a very focused form of exercise that helps to strengthen the body without adding muscle bulk. Over time, it helps to develop a sculpted, toned physique.

Pilates is based on the idea that bad habits or injuries lead to imbalance and weakness in the body. Controlled, repetitive actions are used to realign and re-educate the body. Mental focus and breathing techniques are used to encourage graceful movements and improved awareness.

The Pilates system was created by Joseph Pilates in the early 20th century. Pilates developed an interest in fitness during a sickly childhood in Germany. He studied many forms of exercise, including yoga, gymnastics and body-building, in order to improve his health. Eventually, Pilates used his knowledge and understanding of how the body works to create his own method, which he said could rehabilitate an injured body or strengthen a healthy one.

Pilates exercises have been modified over the years, but teachers hold true to the fundamental ideas of Joseph Pilates. They emphasize the importance of "core strength"

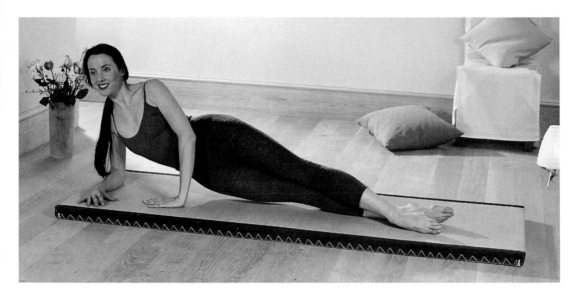

– a stable centre – as well as good alignment and posture. Concentration and controlled breathing help to make Pilates an effective method of relaxation as well as physical fitness.

Yoga-Pilates: an integrated system

You can combine yoga and Pilates to create a fitness programme tailored to your individual needs. Yoga and Pilates naturally share many features. For example, some Pilates exercises are based on yoga poses, and both practices emphasize the importance of good breathing, awareness, and of working within your own abilities.

Yoga-Pilates aims to take the best from both methods, combining the core strength that is the fundamental idea of Pilates with the flexibility and versatility of yoga.

In a sense, you can use Pilates to form a firm foundation on which to build with yoga. In practice, this might mean warming up with Pilates, then moving on to a series of yoga postures in one session. The book provides several sequences that you can use and adapt as you become more aware of your body's needs and strengths.

You don't need to know yoga or Pilates in order to do yoga-Pilates; however if you are already a student of one or the other, yoga-Pilates can show you new ways of working your mind and body. For example, practising Pilates may bring extra strength and stability to your yoga, while incorporating yoga into your Pilates workout can help with relaxation and breathing.

right In yoga, great attention to detail is needed to perfect your alignment. Practising Pilates may help to bring added strength to your practice, and enable you to target specific areas of weakness.

above Practising Pilates at home means that you can adapt your session depending on how you feel on the day. Sometimes you may need a quiet, restful practice; at others, you may want to extend yourself further.

Stay motivated

Almost everyone who exercises admits that it can be difficult to keep motivated. This book aims to give you the greatest possible choice and flexibility, so that you can develop the right exercise programme. Once you have developed an understanding of your body, you'll be able to take elements from the different disciplines, and create workouts to meet your needs and even to suit your mood. Whether you want to calm your mind, improve your posture, tone your muscles or simply enhance your general well-being, it's entirely up to you.

Iyengar Yoga

Judy Smith | CLASSIC YOGA POSTURES FOR MIND, BODY AND SPIRIT

Introduction

Anyone can practise yoga. No matter what level of fitness or ability you have, you can enjoy the benefits of this ancient discipline. Yoga is a good way of improving and maintaining good health, but it works on much more than just the body. Conceived as a form of spiritual training, the main aim of yoga is to create harmony between the mind, body and spirit. It is worth noting that the word yoga is Sanskrit for union.

Much of what we know about the philosophy of yoga comes from a text called the Yoga Sutras, written about 2000 years ago by the Indian sage Patanjali. He described yoga as an eight-fold path to enlightenment. Physical postures (*asana*), breathing exercises (*pranayama*) and meditation (*dhyana*) are all aspects of this spiritual pathway.

Patanjali described how we can transform ourselves through the practice of yoga, gaining control over the mind and emotions and overcoming obstacles to self-realization. At the highest level of practice, we can transcend human consciousness and achieve oneness with the universe.

Yoga in the West

There are many different ways to study yoga. In the West, the spiritual aspects are not usually stressed, and most methods focus on the physical and mental benefits of the asanas. Good breathing is an integral part of the practice; specific pranayama exercises can also be studied, usually once the physical asanas have been mastered. Some teachers also teach meditation practices.

The yoga method covered here is Iyengar, one of the most popular forms. Iyengar yoga is distinguished from other methods by its precision and attention to detail. The main focus is the correct alignment of the body, but the benefits of Iyengar are not limited to the physical. All yoga postures are tools that can be used to bring the body, mind, nerves, consciousness and inner self into harmony.

The Iyengar method

This popular form of yoga was developed in the 20th century by B.K.S. Iyengar. He used his deep understanding of the human body – gained from years of practice – to create a method that is safe, methodical and precise.

In Iyengar yoga, students are taught to pay great attention to getting the pose exactly right, from the position of the foot to the gaze of the eye. Like ballet dancers, they

above In yoga, tiny details such as the interlocking of your fingers can influence the overall effect of an asana. The Iyengar method emphasizes the benefits of focusing on all areas of alignment.

practise the poses over and over again, using all their awareness and concentration to perfect them. The discipline required to achieve this perfect alignment of the body means that the mind, too, becomes focused and sharp.

For all its stress on alignment, the Iyengar method recognizes that everyone's body is different, and that we all have strengths and weaknesses. B.K.S. Iyengar encourages students to work with their own abilities, and to go at their own pace. In addition, props are used to help students to achieve the best possible poses without straining. For example, you may practise a twist on a chair or you may raise the buttocks on a block in order to help you bend forwards without slumping.

The postures

There are five kinds of yoga posture: standing, seated, twisting, inverted (upside-down) and supine or prone (lying down). The poses have a cumulative effect on the body, so it is important that they are practised in the right order.

- Standing asanas build a strong foundation. They help to develop strength, stamina and determination – qualities that can be carried into the other postures. The standing asanas help practitioners to gain awareness of their bodies, and learn to use them intelligently.
- Seated postures improve flexibility of the hips, knees and ankles. They reduce tension in the diaphragm and throat, making breathing smoother. Forward bends are calming poses that soothe the nerves and quieten the mind.
- Twists extend and rotate the spine. They are good for relieving backache and stiffness in the neck and shoulders. The internal organs are stimulated as the trunk turns, which aids the digestion. As the spine becomes more supple, blood flow to the nerves in the spine improves, and energy levels are raised.
- Inverted postures, such as headstands, revitalize the entire body system. The brain is nourished by the blood

above Regular yoga practice is a way of allowing yourself time and space. Once on your mat, you can let go of worries, and allow your mind and body to work in perfect harmony.

that flows towards it. Since there is no weight on the lower body, inversions also bring relief to tired legs.
- Prone (lying down) postures stretch the abdomen and increase flexibility in the spine and hips. Some are restful, while others strengthen the back, arms and legs.

Most routines start with standing postures, to energize the body and remove tension. Seated postures are introduced next, followed by twists, then inversions. Prone and supine postures are usually done at the end of a practice session, which should always be closed with relaxation postures.

Although anyone can practise yoga, it is important to realise that not everyone can do all the poses. Some asanas, including inversions, are not suitable during menstruation; others are best avoided in certain medical conditions. Always read the safety advice for each pose. If you have an injury, illness or you are pregnant, check with a qualified teacher before practising. You should always talk to your doctor before starting a new fitness programme.

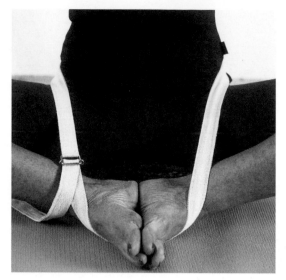

left If your hips are tight, it can be hard to sustain this cobbler pose. Using a belt gives you extra support so that you can relax into the posture and allow tension to drain from the hips and groin.

below Many different props are used in Iyengar classes. It's worth investing in a sticky mat and a strap to use at home. You can also improvise – cushions and folded blankets make good substitutes for bolsters and blocks.

Getting started

Attend a regular yoga class with a qualified Iyengar teacher, so that he or she can help you with your alignment, and also make sure you are progressing at the right rate. Your teacher will also be able to give you individual advice on practising yoga at home.

In general, you should begin by doing just a few postures. It is a good idea to try practising simple standing and sitting routines on alternate days for a few weeks. One day, for example, try the first few standing postures, followed by a standing forward bend, then relaxation. The next, try the first few sitting poses, ending on a simple sitting forward bend. Include the legs up the wall pose to help you rest the body before relaxation.

When you feel comfortable with these asanas, you can put them together in a basic routine. Later on, you can add new postures from each section, making sure that you practise them in the correct order. However, do not be in too much of a hurry to extend your repertoire; the quality and proficiency of your practice is much more important than the number of poses that you do.

Guidelines for practice

It is much better to practise yoga for a short time each day than to do a longer session once or twice a week. The following are some general guidelines for practising yoga:

- Do not eat before a yoga session. Wait at least 4–5 hours after a heavy meal or 2-3 hours after a snack.
- Wear light, loose comfortable clothes that do not restrict your movements. Keep your feet bare. If you wear hard contact lenses, remove them before you start the session. You should also remove jewellery and watches.
- Practise in a warm, airy room out of direct sunlight, on a non-slip floor or, ideally, a yoga mat. Carpet is not suitable, as your feet will slide.
- Always practise with full concentration and awareness. Do the asanas slowly and smoothly, paying attention to accuracy and alignment. Make sure that you do not strain or force the body further than it naturally goes. Over time and with regular practice, you will become more flexible.
- Do not hold your breath. As a general rule, you breathe in on an upward movement, in which the chest and abdomen are expanded, and breathe out on a downward or forward movement, when the chest and abdomen may be compressed. If no indications are given in the instructions for the pose, breathe normally.
- Maintain each pose for as long as possible without causing yourself physical or mental strain. Most people can hold the poses for only a short period at first.

- Where a modification of a pose is given, practise the easier one before attempting the more difficult one for the first time. It is usually best to practise the easy version over a few sessions before progressing onto the next. You may need to stay with the easier version of a pose for a long time, depending on your flexibility.
- Adapt your practice to take account of how you are feeling. For example, if you are tired and lethargic after a long day at work, incorporate more restful forward bends.
- Always end your session, however short, with five to ten minutes relaxation in savasana (corpse pose).
- Be aware that this book is intended as a supplement to classes with an Iyengar teacher, not as a substitute for them. If you suffer adverse physical or mental effects from any pose, stop and seek your teacher's advice.

Using props

Various pieces of equipment can be used to help students get into the asanas more easily and with better alignment. Here are some general guidelines for using props.

- **Non-slip mat** Most yoga students practise on a non-slip mat, which stops the feet from sliding during standing

above Supine postures are done near the end of a yoga session. They have a restorative effect, and lead into relaxation.

postures. You can draw or fold a line down the centre of mat to help you with alignment.
- **Chair** A chair is used for easy twists such as chair pose.
- **Wooden blocks** These are helpful if you cannot reach the floor with your hands in sitting or standing postures. They can also help with twists.
- **Foam blocks** Sitting on foam blocks can lift the spine in seated poses, helping to improve the alignment of the back. Foam blocks can also be used to support the head in restorative poses. You can use one or more folded blankets instead.
- **Bolster** This is used to support the head or spine in restorative poses. A couple of cushions can also be used.
- **Eyebag** A small bean bag can be placed to relax the eyes in recuperative poses.
- **Strap** A strap can be passed around the feet in straight-legged poses if your hands cannot catch the toes or foot. It can also be used to stop the arms sliding apart in shoulder stand, or to secure the feet in cobbler pose.

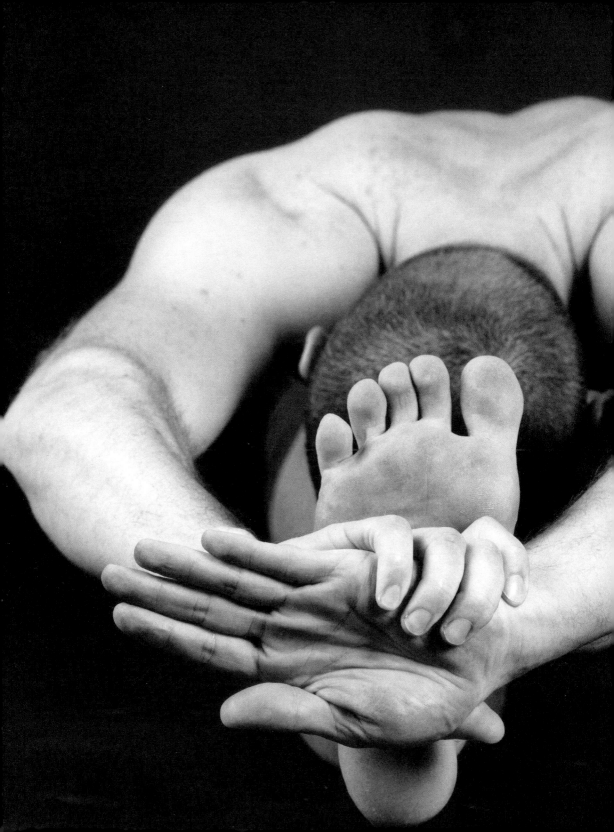

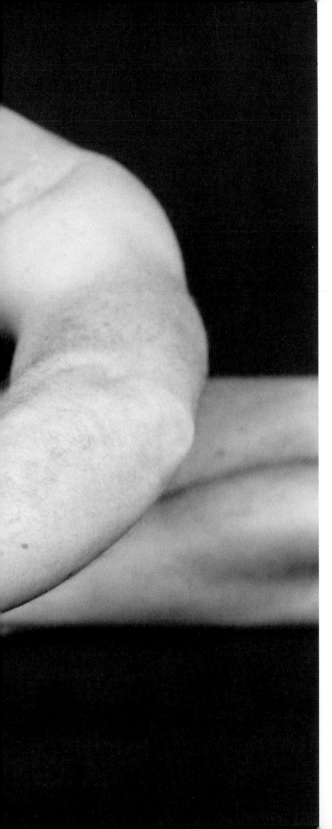

the practice of
Asanas

As you practise yoga, each asana (pose) will become more familiar to you. It's like learning the grammar of a foreign language – little by little, finding your way to the correct pose becomes second nature. Practising the asanas in the right order will help you gain the very most from yoga. Begin with standing and sitting poses, move on to twists and inversions, then do the supine and prone poses. Always end your yoga session with a full relaxation.

Mountain Pose
TADASANA

In this pose we are taught how to stand correctly. It makes us aware of posture, and how the legs and feet have to work in order to stand up straight. All standing poses begin and end with Tadasana.

1 Stand with the feet together – big toes, inner ankles and inner heels touching. Spread the body weight evenly over the feet, keeping the inside edges of the feet parallel.

Tighten/lift the kneecaps and pull up the thigh muscles so the legs stretch strongly. Feel the spine extending upwards and the lift in the front of the body. Roll the shoulders back and take the shoulder blades into the body to open the chest.

2 Allow the arms to hang down the sides of the body with the palms facing the legs.

Extend the neck up, relax the face and look straight ahead. Hold for 30–60 seconds.

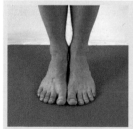

Focus on feet
• It is important to keep the inside edges of the feet parallel, and the big toes and ankle bones together. Weight should be evenly spread over the heels and soles of the feet.

Focus on Tadasana
• Although relatively simple, this posture is crucial as it teaches awareness of the body and the recognition of any postural difficulties. Try to perfect this posture before moving on to the next pose.
• Press the feet firmly into the floor and extend the crown of the head towards the ceiling.
• Extend the sides and back of the neck, balancing the head on the top of the spine.
• Feel the front body "opening" from pubis to chin.
• Project the breastbone towards the front of the chest.
• Ensure that the body is stretching evenly on all sides – front, back, left and right. Strain is caused to the body by leaning habitually to one side or the other.

Modification
• If you find it hard to balance, try Tadasana standing against a wall. This is also helpful to ensure that you are standing straight, and not leaning forwards or backwards.

Tree Pose
VRKSASANA

This posture tones and stretches the leg muscles and teaches balance. Consistent practice of this balancing posture will improve concentration and increases muscle tone and general poise.

1 Stand in Tadasana – feet together, eyes still.

2 Bend the right knee to the side (without disturbing the left leg). Hold the ankle and place the sole of the right foot high on the left inner thigh with the toes pointing towards the floor. Keep the bent (right) knee back in line with the left leg and keep the left leg steady.

3 Inhale and stretch the arms over the head with palms facing one another. Straighten the elbows and extend the arms and trunk up.

Join the palms if you can do so without bending the elbows, otherwise keep them apart. Hold for 30–60 seconds. Exhale, then lower the arms and the right leg and repeat on the other side.

Focus
• To help maintain balance, try to focus the eyes on an object in the middle distance. Balancing poses such as Vrksasana can contribute to improving concentration in the long term.

Modification
• To help with balance, use the wall for support and hold the foot up with a strap.
• Keep the grounded foot pressing firmly into the floor.
• Don't allow the left leg to bow to the side.

Extended Triangle Pose
UTTHITA TRIKONASANA

This pose strengthens the legs, makes the hips more flexible and relieves backache. When turning the feet, it is important not to turn the hips as well. Start on the right side, then repeat the posture to the left.

1 Stand in Tadasana.

2 Inhale deeply, jump or step* your feet 1–1.2m/3–4ft apart and extend the arms out to the side, keeping the palms facing the floor (* students with back or knee problems should step their feet apart). Ensure that both feet are level with one another, legs extended and straight, knees lifted.

3 Turn your left foot out about 90 degrees (parallel to the side of your mat), and turn your right foot slightly inwards (about 15 degrees). The left heel should be in line with the instep of the right foot. As you turn the right foot in, rotate the right leg outwards, and as you turn the left foot outwards, rotate the whole leg to the left, so that the legs are rotating away from one another. Keep the left knee pulled up and facing in the same direction as the left foot.

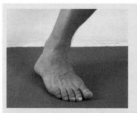 

4 Lift the trunk, extend the arms further and then exhale and stretch the trunk sideways to the left. Hold the left ankle with the left hand.

Extend the right arm upwards, keeping the palm facing forwards and keeping it in line with the left arm. Turn the head and look towards the right thumb.

Extend both legs strongly and rotate the navel forwards and upwards. Hold for 30–40 seconds, inhale and come up. Turn the right foot out and the left foot inwards and repeat on the other side. Come back to the centre in Tadasana.

Focus
• Turn the back foot in 15 degrees. Press the corners of both feet into the floor and lift the instep.
• Stretch the toes forwards and the heels back to lengthen the soles of the feet.
• Do this posture against a wall to aid balance, and, if the neck aches when turning the head, either look straight ahead or look towards the left foot.

Extended Lateral Angle Pose
UTTHITA PARSVAKONASANA

This posture strengthens legs and spine, and helps to open the chest. The full lunge twists the body, stimulating the internal organs, aiding digestion and eliminating toxins.

1 Stand in Tadasana with feet together.

2 Inhale deeply, jump or step your feet 1.3m/4.5ft apart and extend the arms out to the side, keeping the palms facing the floor. Next, turn the right foot inwards 15 degrees and the left foot outwards 90 degrees. Broaden the palms and extend the whole arm from the tops of the shoulders to the fingertips. Move the shoulders away from the ears.

3 Keep the right leg firm and straight, and bend the left knee to 90 degrees – keeping the shin perpendicular and the thigh parallel to the floor. Exhale and extend the trunk sideways, placing the fingertips of the left hand on the floor by the outer edge of the left foot. Lift the right hand up to the ceiling. Keep the right leg stretched and firm – to do this press the outer edge of the right foot into the floor.

4 Turn the right arm towards the head and extend this arm over the head with the palm facing the floor. Turn the head to look towards the ceiling.

Fully extend the right leg and arm and turn the navel towards the ceiling.

Breathe normally and stay in this position for 30–40 seconds. Inhale and come up, turn both feet forwards, rest hands on hips and then repeat the posture on the right side.

After finishing both sides, come back to Tadasana in the centre of your mat.

Focus
• As with all directional postures, begin with the right side first, then continue with the left for balance.
• If the neck is uncomfortable, look straight ahead, not towards the ceiling.
• Move the buttock of the left (bent) leg forwards towards the left inner thigh and, at the same time, keep the left knee moving back slightly, so the groin is open.
• Keep the top arm pointing towards the ceiling, as this will help to keep the chest open and lifted.
• Make sure that the back foot is turned in by 15 degrees and the instep is in line with the heel of the front foot.

Modification
• Place a wooden block under the left hand to open the chest more.
• Do the posture against a wall to improve alignment.

Warrior Pose II
VIRABHADRASANA II

This pose strengthens the legs, brings flexibility to the spinal muscles and tones the abdominal muscles. Although this is called the second posture it is practised first as it is less challenging.

1 Stand in Tadasana.
2 Inhale deeply, jump or step your feet 1–1.2m/3–4ft apart and extend the arms out to the side, palms facing the floor.

3 Keeping your torso facing forwards, turn the right foot out so that it points the same way as your right arm, and turn the left foot in 15 degrees.

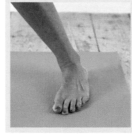

Focus
• Make sure that the back foot is turned in 15 degrees.
• Firmly press the outer edge and the heel of the back foot into the floor to create strength and stability in the back leg.

4 Extend the trunk up from the hips and, as you exhale, bend the right leg to 90 degrees, keeping the left leg firm and straight. Extend the arms strongly to the right and left with the palms facing the floor, stretch the trunk upwards, open the chest, turn the head and look along the right arm.

Extend the left arm more to the left so that the trunk doesn't lean towards the right. The crown of the head should be extending straight up towards the ceiling.

Open the chest, relax the face and breathe normally. Hold for 30–40 seconds, inhale and come up. Turn the feet forwards and repeat on the other side.

After completing both sides, come back into Tadasana.

Modification
• Lean the back of the body against the wall for better alignment.
• Alternatively, place the back heel against the wall, with the fingertips of the back hand touching the wall.

Warrior Pose I
VIRABHADRASANA I

This is a challenging pose in which the chest is well expanded, which in turn improves breathing. It also helps with stiffness in the shoulders, back and neck.

1 Stand in Tadasana, inhale deeply, jump or step the feet 1–1.2m/3–4ft apart and raise the arms to shoulder level.
2 Turn the palms upwards and extend the arms towards the ceiling, keeping the elbows straight and the palms facing one another. If your lower back aches when taking the arms up, then keep your hands on your hips.

3 Turn the right foot and leg in deeply, about 45 degrees, and the left foot out 90 degrees. Simultaneously turn the hips, trunk and shoulders to the left.

Both sides of the trunk should be parallel – so bring the right hip forwards, while taking the left hip slightly back, to keep them even.

Focus
• Don't strain or hold the breath in this posture. Breath is energy, so breathe evenly.

4 Exhale and bend the left leg to form a 90-degree angle. Extend the trunk upwards, as if it were being lifted out of the hips. Move the shoulder blades into the body to open the chest. Extend the chin towards the ceiling and look up. Maintain the full extension on the back leg and keep the hips, shoulders and trunk rotating to the left. Hold for 20–30 seconds, inhale, come up and lower the arms. Repeat on the other side, coming back to Tadasana.

Modification
• If difficulty is experienced in turning the back foot inwards 60 degrees, either work with the back heel against a wall, or support the back heel with a foam block used as a raise.
• If the lower back is uncomfortable, do the pose with the hands on the hips.

Half Moon Pose
ARDHA CHANDRASANA

This pose strengthens the legs and helps improve balance, concentration and co-ordination. Because of the strong extension of the spine, it helps correct alignment and makes the back supple.

1 Start in Tadasana, then move into the full pose for Utthita Trikonasana.
2 Bend the left knee and place the left hand about 30cm/1ft beyond the outer edge of the left foot. Bring the weight of the body on to this foot, using the hand to maintain balance.

3 Exhale and draw the right foot slightly in towards the left leg. Straighten the left leg and the right leg will lift up.

4 Raise and extend the right leg, keeping it parallel to the floor. Keep the left leg firm and pulled up and ensure that it is perpendicular to the floor.

If you are confident with the balance, extend the right arm up towards the ceiling, keeping it in line with the left arm.

Slowly turn the head to look at the right hand and open the chest, lifting the ribs upwards by twisting the waist.

Hold for 20–30 seconds, breathing normally, then come up and repeat on the second side. After finishing both sides, come back to Tadasana.

Focus
• Keep the top hip (the one facing the ceiling) directly above the bottom hip (of the standing leg).
• If the neck is stiff, look ahead, not towards the top hand and the ceiling.

Modification
• If balancing is difficult, do the posture with the back of the body against the wall.
• Use a wooden block as support for the left hand or rest the foot of the lifted leg on a ledge or stool, using blocks to achieve the correct height.

Intense Side Chest Stretch
PARSVOTTANASANA

This calming pose helps to maintain mobility in the neck, shoulders, arms, elbows and wrists. It improves flexibility in the spine and hips, and strengthens the abdominal organs, improving digestion.

1 Stand in Tadasana, and join the hands behind in Namaskar. Inhale and jump or step the feet 1–1.2m/3–4ft apart.
2 Turn the right foot out 90 degrees and the left foot in 45 degrees. Turn the hips, trunk and shoulders to the right.

3 Extend the spine forwards. Lift the chin towards the ceiling and look up to make the back concave.

Focus
• Keep the palms flat together behind the back. This will increase flexibility in the wrists and shoulders.
• Press both feet equally into the floor to relieve pressure on the front leg.

Modification
• Until stability is learned, do the posture with the hands on the waist and, after coming forwards, place the hands on the floor on either side of the front foot.
• If, on first attempting Namaskar, the palms cannot join, hold the elbows behind the back.
• If the back is painful, place each hand on a wooden block after coming forwards, and then extend down.

4 Exhale and extend the trunk over the right leg, taking the head towards the right foot. Keep both legs poker straight, the hips level and the weight evenly distributed between both feet. Hold for 30–40 seconds, raise the trunk, turn the feet forwards, release the hands and repeat on the other side. Come back to the centre of the mat in Tadasana.

Forward Extension
UTTANASANA I

In this pose the spine is given an intense stretch. The abdominal organs are toned and, because the head is down, the increased flow of blood soothes the brain cells. It also relieves fatigue.

1 Stand in Tadasana with the feet 30cm/1ft apart. The inner edges of the feet should be parallel to one another and the toes level. Keep the legs and knees straight.
2 Fold the arms, catching the left elbow with the right hand and the right elbow with the left hand. Inhale and extend the folded arms above the head in line with the ears. Lift and extend the entire body upwards.

3 Exhale and extend the trunk forwards, bending from the waist. Keep the legs lifting upwards, with the weight equally balanced between the feet.

4 Extend the trunk down to the floor, keeping the legs straight, and extend the trunk and arms nearer to the floor. Inhale, lift the trunk, release the elbows and come back to Tadasana.

Focus
• This is a relaxing forward bend. Keep the legs strong and allow gravity to do the rest of the work for you.
.• Keep the legs extending upwards, with the knees lifted, to elongate the spine and protect the lower back.

Modification
• For students with a stiff or painful back and tight hamstring muscles, do supported Uttanasana I – put the hands onto a support at hip level, and extend the spine forwards. An alternative is to rest the head on a support, such as a Halasana stool softened with a blanket.
• If the back is uncomfortable in the final posture, take the feet wider apart and turn the toes slightly inwards.

Forward Extension Legs Wide Apart
PRASARITA PADOTTANASANA

This pose is usually practised towards the end of the standing poses. Because the head is down, increased blood flows to the trunk and head, quietening the body and mind, and promoting tranquillity and serenity.

1 Stand in Tadasana.
2 Inhale and jump or step the feet 1.2–1.5m/4–5ft apart. Make sure the toes of each foot are level and the feet are parallel.

3 Straighten the legs by pulling up the knees and thigh muscles. Exhale and extend the trunk forwards from the hips, stretching the spine.

Place the fingertips on the floor, shoulder-width apart, directly under the shoulders.

Straighten the arms, stretch the legs and extend the trunk forwards, making the back concave and extending the front of the body from the pubis to the chin. Look up.

4 Bend the elbows back, extend the trunk to the floor and place the crown of the head on the floor. Lift the shoulders to release the head nearer to the floor, breathe normally and hold for 20–30 seconds. Inhale, lift the head and trunk to make the back concave. Place the hands on the hips and come back to Tadasana.

Modification
• If the hands don't reach the floor, support each hand with a wooden block.
• If the head doesn't reach the floor, support the crown of the head with foam or wooden blocks.

Focus
• Move the inner thigh muscles away from each other, i.e. inner thighs move towards outer thighs.
• Press the outer edges of both feet into the floor without letting the outer ankle bones bulge down.

• Even though the trunk moves forwards and then down, keep both legs stretching up towards the ceiling.
• Keep the sitting bones in line with your heels. This will stop the legs from leaning forwards or backwards.

Staff Pose
DANDASANA

This is the basic posture for seated poses and forward bends.
It teaches how to sit up straight and extend the spine up.

1 Sit on a raise with the legs stretched out in front. Keep the legs and feet together. Tighten the thigh muscles and knees and extend the heels forwards and extend the toes up towards the ceiling. Place the fingertips on the floor behind the hips, press into the floor and extend the trunk up. Don't overarch the lumbar spine. Roll the shoulders back, open the chest. Look straight ahead and relax the eyes. Move the shoulders away from the ears and the shoulder blades towards the front of the body.

Focus
• Balance the head on the spine centrally.
• Open the ribcage.
• Press the backs of the legs into the floor. Extend the inner heels away from the body, keeping feet upright.

Simple Cross Legs
SUKHASANA

This posture keeps the knees and ankles flexible and nourishes the abdominal organs by encouraging blood circulation in the lower back and the abdomen. Since the spine is erect, the mind stays alert.

1 Sit on a foam block in Dandasana. Cross the legs – place the left foot under the right thigh, and tuck the right foot under the left thigh. Press the fingertips into the floor in order to lift the trunk.
2 Extend the spine up, take the shoulders back and open the chest. Maintain the extension of the spine and put the hands on the knees. Hold for 30–60 seconds.
NOTE: Less flexible students can practise Sukhasana with the back against the wall, extending the spine up the wall.

3 Change the cross-over of the legs so that the other shin-bone is in front and repeat, extending the spine and then placing the hands on the knees again.
Soften the groin area so that the knees release down towards the floor. Note which shin-bone is in front. Cross the shins and keep them in line with the centre of the body.

Hero Pose
VIRASANA

This pose stretches the tops of the feet, ankles and knees. It helps to relieve leg cramps and is a good remedy for indigestion. Because of the position of the feet, it helps to correct flat feet, improving comfort.

1 Kneel on a blanket or yoga mat with the knees together, the feet hip-width apart and the toes pointing straight back behind you.

2 Sit between the feet, using the fingers to move the calf muscles away.

NOTE: If you cannot reach the floor comfortably, use a foam block or rolled-up blanket to raise you up, using as much support as is needed to alleviate knee pain.

3 Put the palms of the hands on the soles of the feet (fingers pointing towards the toes) and stretch the trunk up.

Take the shoulder blades into the body, lift the chest and extend the spine up.

Hold for 1–2 minutes, come out of the pose and straighten the legs.

Hero Pose Forward Bend
ADHO MUKHA VIRASANA

This resting posture helps to soothe and calm the brain, relieve fatigue and headaches, stretch and tone the spine, and ease back and neck pain.

1 Kneel on a blanket with the big toes together and the knees hip-width apart. Sit on the heels with the buttocks, so that the tailbone end of the spine is supported.

Once the buttocks are down, extend the trunk forwards and put the forehead on the floor. Stretch both arms and the sides of the trunk forwards, and put the palms on the floor. Don't take the knees too far apart.

Modification

• The tailbone must be supported on the heels. If this cannot be done, put a foam block between the buttocks and the heels.

• If the forehead cannot reach the floor, rest it on a foam block or a folded blanket.

Hero Pose with Extended Arms
VIRASANA WITH PARVATASANA

Parvatasana creates movement in the shoulder joints and develops the muscles of the chest. When the arms are raised, the abdominal organs are drawn in and the chest lifts and opens.

1 Sit in Virasana (or in Sukhasana if you find Virasana difficult) and interlock the fingers with the right index finger over the left.

Turn the palms outwards, so that they face away from your body. Stretch the arms forwards, keeping them parallel to the floor and straightening the elbows. Keep the spine stretching upwards from the base of the pelvis.

2 Extend the arms up with the elbows straight. The upper arms are in line with the ears and the palms are facing the ceiling.

Don't overarch in the lower back – extend the trunk and arms strongly upwards. Hold for 30–60 seconds, lower the arms, change the interlock of the fingers (i.e. left index finger over right) and repeat.

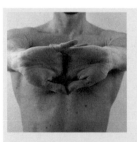

Focus
• Clasp the hands at the root of the fingers and, when extending the arms up, don't allow the fingers to slide apart.
• Change the interlock of the fingers half-way through this pose.

Modification
• If there is difficulty clasping the hands together due to stiffness in the shoulders, then use a strap. Practising this pose will help to relieve the problem.
• If the tops of the feet are painful, put them on a rolled-up blanket.

Head of Cow Pose
GOMUKHASANA (ARMS ONLY)

Gomukhasana expands the chest and brings flexibility to the wrists, and to the shoulders. As the spine extends strongly upwards, the shoulder joints become less restricted and the shoulder muscles are fully stretched.

1 Sit in Dandasana and extend the right arm.

2 Bend the right arm behind the back and take the forearm up the back with the palm facing outwards.

4 Extend the left arm up, turn the palm back, bend the elbow, put the palm of the hand below the nape of the neck and clasp the right hand.

3 Use the left hand to bring the right elbow closer to the trunk, so that the right hand moves farther up the back.

5 Roll the right shoulder back and stretch the left elbow towards the ceiling. Keep the trunk upright and look straight ahead. Hold for 30–60 seconds and repeat on the other side.

Modification
• Use a strap if the hands cannot grasp one another.
• Keep both sides of the trunk at an equal length and keep the head straight and the eyes level. Don't overarch the lower back.

Head to Knee Pose
JANUSIRSASANA

Janusirsasana stimulates the digestive system, tones the abdominal muscles and brings the brain and heart into a restful state. Forward bends are beneficial for a good night's sleep.

1 Sit in Dandasana on a support, bend the left knee to the side and place the left foot so that the sole of the foot is parallel to the right thigh.
2 Inhale and extend both arms straight up to the ceiling, moving the shoulder blades into the body. The upper arms are beside the ears. Stretch the spine upwards.

3 Exhale, bend forwards and catch the sides of the right foot with both hands. Make the spine concave and look up. If the lower back aches, do not proceed any further.

4 Exhale, widen the elbows out to the side, extend the trunk further forwards and take the head down.
  Hold for 30–60 seconds, inhale, release the foot, come up and repeat on the other side.

Focus
• Keep the right leg straight with the toes pointing up. Press the back of the right leg down on to the floor.

Modification
• If you can't reach the right foot, use a strap around the foot, holding it in a "V" shape with both hands.
• If you are able to catch the foot, hold it around the sides of the foot, not the toes.
• If the lower back is painful, rest the forehead on a stool or bolster.
• Sit on a foam block and support the bent knee on a foam block if it is uncomfortable.

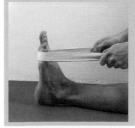 

Full Forward Bend
PASCIMOTTANASANA

This posture tones and activates the abdominal organs, aids digestion and rejuvenates the spine. As the body is in a horizontal position in forward bend poses, there is less strain on the heart.

1 Sit in Dandasana on a support.
2 Inhale, extend the arms up (palms facing), keeping the upper arms besides the ears.

3 Exhale, extend the trunk forwards, clasp the sides of both feet with the hands (or use a strap). Inhale and extend forwards, make the back concave, lift the chest and look up.

Modification
• If the backs of the knees are painful when pressed into the floor, place a rolled-up blanket under the knees.
• If the forehead cannot reach the legs, rest it on a foam block or a folded blanket.
• In cases of extreme stiffness, or pain in the back, rest the head on a stool covered with a blanket.

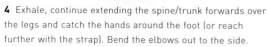

4 Exhale, continue extending the spine/trunk forwards over the legs and catch the hands around the foot (or reach further with the strap). Bend the elbows out to the side.

Fully extend the front of the body and the sides of the trunk. Take the head down. If the back aches, rest the head on a bolster or stool. Hold for 30–60 seconds, inhale and come up.

Focus
• Press the back of the legs down into the floor to extend the spine more.
• Extend the inner heels away, with toes stretching towards the ceiling.
• Pull on the feet or the strap to lengthen the trunk.

Standing Twist
STANDING MARICYASANA

This posture reduces stiffness in the neck and shoulders. It improves the alignment of the spine and strengthens the spinal muscles. It also relieves lower back pain and sciatica.

1 Put a stool near the wall. Stand in Tadasana with the wall on your right. Bend the right knee and place the foot on the stool, keeping the right thigh against the wall.

Inhale, stretch the left leg strongly up and keep the toes of this foot facing forwards. Extend the trunk towards the ceiling. Exhale, turn the front body to face the wall, and place the hands on the wall at shoulder level.

Inhale, extend the trunk further, exhale, press the hands into the wall to enable the trunk to turn more to the right. Turn as far as you can, look over the right shoulder. Hold for 20–40 seconds, release, and repeat on the other side.

Focus
• Don't allow the front body to lean towards the wall.
• Move the shoulder blades into the body and downwards towards the waist to open the chest.

Easy Pose Twist
SUKHASANA (TWIST)

In this easy, cross-legged twist, use the breath to lift and turn. Relax the shoulders, moving them away from the ears and into the body.

1 Sit in step 1 of Sukhasana, with the fingertips on the floor.
2 Place the palm of the left hand on the outer right thigh. Inhale, press the right fingertips into the floor and extend the spine upwards. Exhale, press the left palm into the thigh
and turn towards the right.
3 Look over the right shoulder. Hold for 30–40 seconds, release and repeat on the other side, changing the cross of the legs.

Simple Twist Using a Chair
BHARADVAJASANA (CHAIR)

In this twist, the chair is used to allow a safe and effective rotation of the trunk. It makes the muscles of the spine supple, relieves stiff neck and shoulders, improves digestion and exercises the abdominals.

1 Sit on a chair with the right side of the body facing the chair-back. Keep the knees and feet together. Sit up straight and look straight ahead.
2 Inhale, extend the spine up and put the hands on the back of the chair.

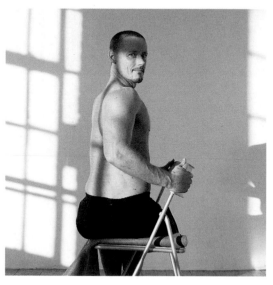

3 Exhale, and turn the trunk to the right, using the hands to help you turn.
  Inhale, lift the spine further, take the shoulder blades into the body and open the chest. Rotate the spine further so that the chest is parallel to the back of the chair. Keep the neck free from tension or strain.

Focus
- Press both feet firmly into the floor to lift the trunk.
- Press the left buttock down towards the seat of the chair – it wants to lift. Use the inhalation to extend the spine; use the exhalation to turn it.

Modification
- This twist can be made easier by raising the feet, or by placing a block between the knees.

4 Exhale, turn the trunk more and look over the right shoulder. Grip the back of the chair for leverage. Hold for 20–30 seconds, exhale, release the hands, face forwards and repeat on the other side.

Legs Up the Wall Pose
VIPARITA KARANI

This restorative pose calms the brain, opens the chest and rests the legs. It helps reduce respiratory problems, eases headaches and relieves indigestion and nausea. It also helps to prevent varicose veins.

NOTE: Women should NOT practise any inversions during menstruation, as these asanas will interfere with the natural flow of blood at this time.

1 Put a wooden block against the wall with a bolster in front and a folded blanket in front of the bolster.

2 Sit on the bolster, sideways to the wall with the hip touching the wall.

3 Swivel the trunk around, using the hands to balance. Take one leg up the wall, keep the buttocks against the wall and straighten the second leg.

4 Once both legs are up the wall, carefully take the trunk down and lower the shoulders and head on to the floor. Keep the backs of the legs and buttocks against the wall and open the chest.

Focus
• Keep the inner edges of the feet together so that the soles of the feet are parallel to the ceiling.
• Keep the abdomen soft and press the shoulders into the floor.

5 Take the arms over the head, breathe evenly and relax. Hold for 5–6 minutes and then come down.

Shoulder Stand Bridge Pose
SETU BANDHA SARVANGASANA (SUPPORTED)

This pose opens the chest and gives a mild extension to the spine. It calms the brain, reduces depression and relieves headaches. The abdominal muscles are stretched and strengthened, improving digestion.

1 Lie on the floor with the knees bent and the toes pointing towards the wall.
2 Keeping the head, neck and shoulders on the floor, press the feet down and lift the hips from the floor. Put a wooden block vertically under the sacrum near the tailbone.

3 Straighten one leg at a time and place the feet on the wall at whatever height is comfortable for the lower back.

Modification
• If the wooden block is uncomfortable on the sacrum (lower back), use four stacked foam blocks.
• If the lower back hurts, support the feet on wooden blocks or a bolster.

4 Open the chest, and extend the arms towards the feet, which are pressing firmly into the wall. Roll the tops of the shoulders towards the floor and move the shoulder blades towards the front of the body to open the chest.

Hold for 1–2 minutes, bend the legs, remove the block and come down.

Focus
• Maintain a strong stretch on the back of the legs from the buttock bones to the heels.
• There should be no tension in the neck.
• Lift the breastbone towards the chin.

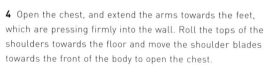

Supported Shoulder Stand
SALAMBA SARVANGASANA

This posture soothes and nourishes the internal organs, helps the thyroid gland to function and frees the body of toxins. It is beneficial for relieving respiratory problems such as asthma, congestion and sinusitis.

NOTE: Women should NOT practise any inversions during menstruation, as these asanas will interfere with the natural flow of blood at this time.

1 Place four small, or one large, foam block and a folded blanket on the mat for comfort. Lie with the shoulders and arms on the support and the head on the floor.

Stretch the arms towards the feet and move the shoulders away from the head.

2 Inhale and bring your legs and hips up. Bend the knees towards the chest. Keep the spine straight and do not move the head or neck. Press the fingertips into the floor, and take the knees towards the head. Keep the movement steady and controlled at all times.

3 Lift the hips and trunk and immediately support the back with the palms of both hands. Straighten the legs and move the hands up the back towards the shoulder blades to increase the lift of the chest. Bring the chest towards the chin and stretch the whole body straight up. Look towards the chest. Hold for 2–5 minutes.

Focus
• Press the hands into the back to move the back ribs towards the front of the chest and to lift the trunk. Press the upper arms into the support.

Modification
• Tie a belt under the upper arms, just above the elbows, to keep them shoulder-width apart.
• Stretch the legs up and keep the soles of the feet parallel to the ceiling. Rest the toes on a wall, if easier.

Half Plough Pose
ARDHA HALASANA

This supported version of Halasana is a restorative pose. It reduces the effects of fatigue, anxiety and insomnia, and relieves stress-related headaches.

1 Place a chair/stool over the head before going into Salamba Sarvangasana. From this pose, take the legs down on to the stool to support the thighs.
2 Straighten the legs and support the spine with the hands.
3 Take the arms over the head and relax. Hold for 2–5 minutes, bend the knees, slide the thighs off the stool and come down.

Plough Pose
HALASANA

This inversion relaxes the brain, and improves the functioning of the thyroid and parathyroid glands. It is beneficial to practise it when one has a cold.

1 Go into Salamba Sarvangasana with the shoulders on a folded blanket or foam support. Take the legs down over the head to the floor and put the feet on the floor.

Keep supporting the back with the hands, lift the back and keep the chest open and lifted. Straighten the legs, extending them away from the hips.

Relax the eyes, hold for 2–5 minutes and come down.

Modification
• If the back hurts, put a support under the toes.
• The tips of the toes press into the floor or bricks. Lift thigh bones towards the ceiling and stretch the heels away from the head.

Fish Pose
MATSYASANA (SIMPLE)

Here the muscles of the spine and abdomen are fully stretched. Flexibility in the hips, knees and ankles develops and the chest lifts and opens, so the depth of the breath improves.

1 Sit in Sukhasana, crossing the right shin-bone over the left.
2 Lean back by resting on the elbows and then lie down. Soften the groin to allow the knees to release towards the floor. **NOTE**: If the groin is painful, support each knee with a foam block or bolster.

Focus
• Cross the legs evenly at the shins, not at the ankles, and change the cross.
• Don't overarch in the lower back – lengthen it by extending the sacrum towards the feet.

3 Take the arms over the head, straighten the elbows and extend the arms strongly back.
   Extend the trunk towards the head and the knees away from the head. Keep the lower back long (don't arch it) and move the shoulders away from the floor and towards the ceiling to lift and open the chest.
   Hold for 1–2 minutes, come up, change the cross-over of the legs and repeat.

Cross Bolsters

This pose gently stretches the back and soothes the brain. As the back ribs are supported by the vertical bolster, the chest opens and breathing deepens, the abdomen extends and the whole body relaxes.

1 Place two bolsters on the floor, the first one horizontal and the second lengthways on top. Sit on the top bolster where it crosses over the bottom one, and bend the knees.
2 Lie back, placing the lower back on the highest part of the top bolster and gently lowering the shoulders down on to the floor.
3 Extend the legs forwards, take the arms over the head and relax them.
   Hold for 2–5 minutes, bend the knees, slide back towards the head, roll over to the side and get up.

Modification
• If the lower back aches during this stretch, lift the feet and place on two or three foam blocks.

Supine Cobbler Pose
SUPTA BADDHAKONASANA

This recuperative pose is particularly useful for women, especially during menstruation. The strap around the lower back lengthens the spine, and the bolster lifts the chest. This pose also helps sciatica.

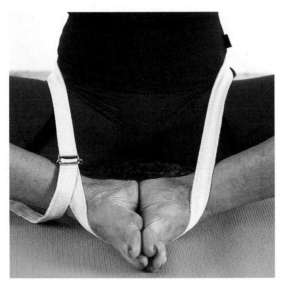

1 Place a bolster lengthways on the floor with a folded blanket at the top end. Sit in front of the bolster with the edge in contact with the lower back. Bend the knees out to the sides, take the soles of the feet together and draw the heels as close to the pubis as possible. Loop the strap across the lower back, over the hips and bind the soles of the feet together at the ankles.

2 Lie back over the bolster, so that the edge is touching the lower back, and support the head and neck with the folded blanket.

Feel the bolster gently moving the spine into the body and the resultant broadening, lifting and opening of the chest. Allow the shoulders to roll down towards the bolster. Keep the face, mouth and throat relaxed.

Release tension from the groin and extend it outwards to the sides. If necessary, use the hands to turn the inner thighs and calves gently upwards to help the knees descend a little further. Relax the ankles and knees.

Take the arms out to the side, keeping the palms facing upwards. Relax them and close the eyes.

Hold for 2–5 minutes, focusing on the breathing, then open the eyes and come up.

Modification
• If the back is aching, put more support on the bolster and under the head.
• If the groin is uncomfortable, support each knee with a foam block or bolster.
• If the back aches in this posture despite the extra support, come out of it and lie over the bolster with the legs crossed as in Sukhasana.

Focus
• Make sure that, once the strap is brought down to the hips, it lies close to the pubic bone, not the waist.
• As you lie back, the strap will keep the feet as close to the body as possible.

Reclining Hero Pose
SUPTA VIRASANA

This pose stretches the abdominal organs and pelvic region, and relieves aching legs. If the back aches despite the extra support, come out of the posture and lie over the bolster with legs crossed.

1 Place a bolster lengthways on a mat with a folded blanket at the top end to support the head. Sit in Virasana on a foam block placed against the bolster.

Hold the bolster against the lower back and lie over the bolster, supporting the head and neck on the folded blanket. Take the arms out to the side, palms facing upwards. Hold for 3–5 minutes and come up.

Modification
• If the knees or lower back are painful, put another bolster under the first one.
• Keep the shoulders back and chest open and raised.
• If necessary, place more blankets under the head.

Legs Stretched to 90 Degrees
URDHVA PRASARITA PADASANA

This pose strengthens the lower back and gives relief to tired legs.
The brain stays calm while focusing on the breath.

1 Sit sideways to the wall and move the right hip and buttock as close to the wall as possible. Lean back, swivel the trunk around and take both legs up the wall. Lift the head to check the alignment; the head should be in line with the tailbone.

Lie down and allow the wall to support the legs. Extend both arms over the head, keep the hips down, and stretch the legs up the wall.

Hold for 40–60 seconds and come up.

Focus
• Extend the backs of the legs towards the ceiling and press them into the wall.
• Keep the lower back and hips moving towards the floor.
• Take the shoulder blades into the body to open the chest.
• This is considered a supine, relaxing pose, while Viparita Karani raises the hips and back off the floor, and is therefore considered an inverted posture.

Prone Leg Stretch
SUPTA PADANGUSTHASANA I & II

Supta Padangusthasana I & II are good for stretching hamstring muscles. Both poses strengthen knees and hip joints, and help to relieve sciatica. The pelvic area is aligned, easing stiffness in the lower back.

1 Lie down on a mat or blanket, with the soles of both feet touching the wall.
2 Bend the right knee towards the chest, and grab the big toe with the thumb and forefinger.

3 Supta Padangusthasana I – Stretch the right leg straight up towards the ceiling while pressing the sole of the left foot more firmly into the wall. Keep the right leg at a 90-degree angle. (If the back is painful, take the leg to a 60-/70-degree angle.)

Lengthen the back of the right leg from the buttock bone to the heel, and feel the extension of the right calf. Press the back of the left leg into, and along, the floor to extend the hamstring muscle. Pull gently on the lifted foot to open the chest.

Hold the pose for 30–40 seconds, come down and repeat with the left leg.

4 Supta Padangusthasana II – follow the instructions as before, extend the leg up to 90 degrees and then stretch the right leg and arm sideways to the right. Take the right leg towards the floor without disturbing the head, trunk or the left leg.

Press the sole of the left foot into the wall and the back of the leg into the floor. If the whole body rolls over towards the right, put a support under the right foot to control the descent of the leg (if using a strap, pull on it with the right hand) and extend the left arm out to the side.

Open the chest. Hold for 30–40 seconds and repeat on the other side.

Modification
• Students with tight hamstrings can use a strap around the foot, rather than catching the big toe.
• If difficulty is experienced with the leg to the side, rest the thigh on a bolster.

Dog Pose
ADHO MUKHA SVANASANA

Dog pose is a good all-over stretch. It extends the legs and strengthens the ankles. It also eases stiffness in the neck, shoulders and wrists. Staying longer in this pose removes fatigue and restores energy.

1 Get on to all fours (hands and knees). Place the palms on the floor, hands shoulder-width apart, with the middle fingers pointing forwards. Take the knees hip-width apart and tuck the toes under.

Press the hands firmly into the floor, particularly the thumbs and index fingers. Fully straighten the arms, extending them from the floor towards the shoulders. Move the shoulders away from the ears and the shoulder blades into the body to open the chest.

2 Come up on to the balls of the feet and raise the hips. Extend the sitting bones towards the ceiling. Straighten the legs and extend the heels towards the floor without losing the lift in the hips. Press the thighs back.

Straighten both elbows, lift the shoulders towards the waist and stretch the trunk upwards. Relax the head towards the floor, keeping the throat and eyes soft. Keep the arms and legs firm.

Hold for 20–30 seconds, bend the knees and come down.

Modification
• For an easier version of this posture, work with the hands or feet supported by a wall.
• Turn the hands out and place the palms on the floor with the index fingers and thumbs against the wall.

• Alternatively, start with the back to the wall, rest the heels up the wall and come into the pose.
• If there is strain in the head or neck, rest the forehead on a bolster for a more restful version of this posture.

Dog Pose (Head Up)
URDHVA MUKHA SVANASANA

This pose strengthens the spine and eases backache and sciatica. Increased blood flow to the pelvic area nourishes the internal organs. The chest expands, and flexibility in the neck and shoulders increases.

1 Lie face down on the floor and stretch both legs back, pressing the tops of the feet into the floor. (If the lower back hurts, tuck the toes under.) Place the palms on the floor beside the chest and spread the fingers.

2 Inhale, raising the head and chest. Lengthen the neck as you extend upwards. Tuck in the sitting bones, and draw the pubic bone towards your chest. Straighten the arms and lock the elbows.

3 Lift the hips, thighs and knees a few centimetres/inches off the floor, bringing the tailbone and sacrum forwards.
  Keeping the elbows straight, roll the shoulders back, lift the chest further and curve the trunk back between the arms. Lengthen the back of the neck, take the head back slightly and look up. Stay in this position for 30–40 seconds, breathing evenly.

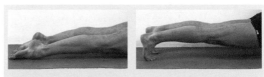

Focus
• Keep the toes pointing backwards, and lift the legs off the floor. If difficulty is experienced lifting the legs off the floor, tuck the toes under and then lift up.
• To lift the trunk and chest more, put each hand on a wooden block.

Corpse Pose
SAVASANA

Also known as Relaxation, this pose helps to release tension in the muscles, and settle the breathing, after performing the asanas. Energy flows into and through the body, recharging it and removing stress.

1 Sit in the centre of the mat with the knees bent and the feet on the floor. Put a folded blanket at the head end of the mat.

2 Lower the trunk down, rest on the elbows and check the body alignment, then carefully lower the trunk on to the floor. Place the centre of the back of the head on the support.

3 Straighten one leg at a time and, when straight, keep the legs and feet together.

Release the tension in the legs and allow the feet to drop out to the side.

4 Stretch the arms out to the side, slightly away from the sides of the trunk. Turn the palms so that the knuckles of the little fingers are touching the floor as much as the knuckles of the index fingers. Relax the hands, allowing the fingertips to curl slightly inwards.

Shut the eyes by lowering the upper eyelids towards the lower eyelids. Relax the eyes and facial features and allow the body to sink into the floor.

Breathe evenly and focus on the breath in order to keep the brain calm and passive. Don't go to sleep.

Hold for 5–10 minutes, slowly open the eyes, bend the knees, roll over to the right side and slowly come up.

Focus
• Let your body go and surrender to the floor.
• Relax the fingers and palms of the hands.
• Keep the head straight, with the bridge of the nose facing the ceiling.
• Relax the thigh muscles and let the legs roll away from one another.

• Keep the arms away from the sides of the body, but be sure that the elbows are not taut. Allow the hands to relax, and let the feeling spread up your arms to the shoulders.
• Draw the organs of perception (eyes, ears and tongue) inwards so that the mind and body become one and inner

Breathing
UJJAYI PRANAYAMA

In Pranayama, the brain becomes quiet which allows the nervous system to function more effectively.
It generates a store of energy in the body, while strengthening and increasing the capacity of the lungs.

1 Normal Inhalation/Extended Exhalation

Lie in Savasana on a bolster or blanket, with another folded blanket under the head. Cover the eyes with a bandage. Spend a few minutes becoming aware of your normal breathing. Exhale, relax the abdomen. Inhale normally.

Exhale slowly, quietly and smoothly, lengthening the breath without straining. Inhale normally again. Exhale slowly, deeply and smoothly.

If breathlessness or fatigue is experienced in between cycles, take a few normal breaths before proceeding. Continue in this manner for 5 minutes. Return to normal breathing to allow the lungs to recover.

Focus

- Keep the face and eyes relaxed during Pranayama.
- Relax the mouth, tongue and throat.
- Keep the chest and ribcage lifted throughout.
- Keep the shoulders moving away from the ears.
- Keep the abdomen soft in inhalation and exhalation.
- Soften the palms of the hands and relax the fingers.
- If the mind is racing, an eye bandage will aid calmness.

2 Extended Inhalation/Normal Exhalation

Exhale, completely emptying air from the lungs.

Take a slow, soft inhalation, filling the lungs from the bottom to the top.

Don't strain or jerk the chest, breathe smoothly and lengthen the breath calmly.

Exhale normally. Inhale once more, slowly drawing the breath into the lungs.

Exhale normally.

Repeat these two cycles for about 5 minutes, then return to normal breathing. Once you've returned to normal breathing, check that there is no tension in the shoulders, throat, mouth or hands.

NOTE: Exercise caution when practising Pranayama – incorrect practice may strain the lungs and diaphragm. Beginners should master the postures and gain control over the body before attempting Pranayama.

These two cycles can be practised separately or together and should be done for a few months before proceeding to breathing with extended inhalation and extended exhalation.

3 Extended Inhalation/Extended Exhalation

Exhale, completely emptying the lungs of air. Inhale slowly and smoothly, lengthening the breath.

Maintain the lift of the chest, and exhale slowly and deeply without straining the throat.

Control the flow of breath so that the body doesn't shudder or strain. Take a few normal breaths. Repeat for about 5 minutes. Return to normal breathing.

To end the above cycles, bend the knees, roll over to the side and remove the bolster. Lie flat, with the head still supported, in Savasana, for 5 minutes, keeping the brain quiet and releasing the body to the floor. Slowly open the eyes, turn to one side, stay for a moment, then turn to the other side. Come up and sit in Adho Mukha Virasana before getting up.

Pilates

Emily Kelly | SIMPLE TECHNIQUES FOR
A STRONG, LITHE,
HEALTHIER BODY

Introducing Pilates

What is it about Pilates that makes it such a favourite in gyms and dance schools and such a respected and popular activity? With all the different exercise videos and books on the market, what makes this technique special?

Maybe the answer can be summed up in one word: commonsense. This section is designed to be an accessible manual that you can integrate into your life. It explains the key elements of Pilates and takes you by the hand through a comprehensive range of exercises. The programme aims to be very user-friendly: it is designed for beginners to Pilates but more advanced variations of many exercises are included so that you can have greater challenges as you progress.

The "first position" in each exercise is the most basic option. If you are new to Pilates then always start with this one, otherwise you will not have mastered the control and the focus needed to perform the exercise correctly. During a Pilates session your main concern should be the feeling that you get from doing the movement correctly, not how many repetitions you can do. The

above Pilates helps to re-define posture, creating a relaxed, confident stance. It is worth remembering that the correct posture can give an illusion of a 6 lb weight loss.

"second position" should only be attemped after you have a clear understanding of the first position. For some people this may take two or more months. For others, it may take as little as three weeks. Everyone is different. It is not a competition, just progress at your own rate. The "third position" is a more intense variation still.

You may find that you progress faster with some exercises than with others. This is perfectly normal. For example, you may have a slight imbalance in your body that is being strongly challenged by the movement. Have faith in your knowledge of how your own body feels.

The holistic approach

This section aims to get you to look at exercise in a holistic way and to help you integrate it into your daily life with only minimal disturbance. It does not set out to turn you into an Olympic athlete. It might, however, give you that little push you need to start exercising by explaining just why it is important, not just for aesthetic purposes but to help you avoid pain and injury, to make you feel good about your body and to increase your self-esteem.

The intention is that you will find the programme clear, logical and simple to remember, so that it will be quite easy to make it a regular part of your daily routine – just like brushing your teeth – because exercise really should be a matter of course. It's just common sense. You need to take care of your body at least as well as you take care of your car. You probably expect your car to last you six or seven years, and oil changes, tune-ups and wheel alignments are common practice for every car owner. How long do you want your body to last you?

Everyone can benefit

So who can benefit from this programme? Basically, Pilates has something to offer everyone, whatever your age or current fitness level. Although you will get stronger all over, one of the main benefits of Pilates is an increase in core strength. This is a phrase that is used over and over again in connection with Pilates, and it refers to the important abdominal and back muscles at your centre that support your whole body whether moving or at rest. As these muscles are strengthened, your posture will improve and you will find it easier to go about your daily tasks.

If you are completely new to Pilates, you will find these exercises different from others you may have tried. First of all, Pilates is a series of movements that flow into one another without pauses. Most conventional exercise starts and stops: you might do 12 repetitions of a move, rest, and then start up again with the next sequence. Pilates concentrates on the body as a whole, stretching some muscles, strengthening

above Pilates combines stretches and strengthening exercises, making it one of the safest and most effective forms of exercise.

right Pilates creates a strong, lean, balanced body. This reduces the risk of injury and helps to elimate nagging aches and pains.

others and, by helping you to function more effectively, reducing the risk of injury, not only while you are exercising but in everything you do.

Many people who take up Pilates are pleased to discover that only a small number of repetitions are needed per exercise in comparison with other conventional methods. If you are performing the movements correctly, up to ten repetitions will be more than adequate. This means that you can give each repetition your full effort and concentration: you will be maximizing the potential of the exercise without growing tired or bored with continual repetitions.

The importance of focus

Another distinguishing feature of Pilates is that to practise it you must be totally focused and concentrated, and this concentration creates a mind-body connection. This doesn't mean that conventional exercise can be done without thought of course, but it does mean that Pilates needs all your attention and focus in order to get the best results. If you sometimes feel overwhelmed by everyday problems and stresses, giving all your attention to the movements of a Pilates sequence can help to still the insistent clamour of your daily life, acting like meditation to calm your mind and help you see things more clearly. This total concentration and attention to alignment and detail makes Pilates quite unique and very satisfying.

Be kind to yourself

When you start the programme, it is important that you do not place any expectations on yourself. Pilates is about the feeling you are getting from the exercise, not about how many repetitions you can do, how long you exercise for or how many advanced exercises you can work through. Some of the movements are very subtle and to an observer it may appear that you are doing very little. You should check throughout the exercises that

below Within weeks of beginning regular Pilates practice, you will see a clear improvement. Pilates creates long, lean muscles with no risk of developing a bulky, overdeveloped physique.

right Pilates should be combined with healthy eating and regular cardiovascular exercise for optimum results.

your spine is in neutral (unless otherwise stated), that the abdominals are contracted, that you are not holding your breath at any time, that the muscles not involved in the movement are relaxed (it is common to hold tension in the jaw and shoulders), and that the movements are controlled. All these factors are the key elements that make Pilates so effective, and they are fully explained on the following pages.

Pilates is a very personal experience. Listen to your body and stop if anything feels uncomfortable or causes pain – though this should not be confused with an exercise being challenging. It could be that a particular exercise is not right for you at this time;

right Pilates should be combined with healthy eating and regular cardiovascular exercise for optimum results.

you can always come back to it on another occasion, or try the less intense version of the same exercise. If you simply cannot focus on an exercise during a session, choose another exercise from the same category; don't waste your time and create negative feeling for a movement.

The endorphin effect

You will sometimes hear regular exercisers talking about the high they get from activity: what they are describing is the production of endorphins, chemicals in the brain that are stimulated by exercise and have similar effects to that of opiates. If you need any more encouragement to get started, consider this: tests have shown that people who suffer from illness and depression are significantly helped by taking exercise.

As well as describing each exercise in detail, the book gives advice on putting together a sequence to help you achieve the benefits you are seeking, and on incorporating Pilates into an all-round fitness regime of exercise and healthy eating. Start investing in the present and future health of your body, today.

left Regular practice of Pilates will help you achieve a long, lean, strong physique.

The History of Pilates

Recently it has become almost impossible to open a magazine and not find mention of a Pilates-based exercise programme. Everyone is talking about this "new" form of exercise, especially having seen the way it has sculpted celebrities such as Courtney Love, Sophie Dahl, Madonna and Melanie Griffiths. We jogged in the 70s, did aerobics with Jane Fonda in the 80s, took up weight-training in the 90s; in the new millennium we are discovering the mind-body experience.

In reality, Pilates has been around for a century. For ballet dancers, it has been a well-kept secret as the perfect way to become strong and centred without building bulk. Only in the past few years has the fitness world embraced Pilates, and this accounts for its sudden and well-deserved popularity as a form of exercise.

Joseph Pilates was born in Germany in 1880. He was a sickly child and suffered from asthma, rickets and rheumatic fever, which left him with a burning desire to become physically stronger. By the age of 14 he was an avid body-builder with a well-sculpted physique. He practised all types of sports, such as skiing, diving and gymnastics. At 32 he moved to England, where he made his living as a boxer, circus performer and self-defence instructor for detectives.

left The Pilates method was originally developed to build strength and increase immunity. Today, the many modified forms of the techniques still teach your body to work at its most efficient.

When World War I broke out Pilates was interned in the Isle of Man. Being such a keen fan of exercise, Pilates decided that his fellow internees should get fit under his training. His efforts paid off, as none of his trainees succumbed to the massive influenza epidemic that killed millions after the war. He also worked as a hospital orderly, encountering many war casualties. He started working with some of the disabled patients, using his own body weight to move their limbs and devising special equipment to aid their progress. This consisted of springs attached to their hospital beds which gave gentle resistance to aid muscle strengthening and stretching: these were the prototypes of the machines that are used today.

Pilates believed that imbalances in the body and habitual patterns of movement cause injuries. He observed the links between weak areas of the body and over-

compensation (if you are weak in one area the rest of the body has to support the imbalance), and the exercises he devised were based around re-education and the re-alignment of the body.

In 1926 Pilates and his wife Clara moved to New York where they set up an exercise studio. By 1940 the dance community had become aware of his fitness programmes, including George Balanchine and other members of the New York City Ballet.

Pilates had a number of students who went on to set up their own studios and so the method spread, each teacher adding their own personal twists, as they continue to do today. It would be rare to find two instructors who teach Pilates in exactly the same way.

Since Pilates' death, followers of his methods have modified the original 34 exercises and made them more user-friendly. The Pilates method is practised in one of two ways: using equipment called a re-former, an updated version of the original springs, or as free body exercises using only a mat. The latter is the version that you will be taught in this section.

left Performing artists, such as singers, dancers, actors and models, have long used Pilates' methods to improve posture, align their body, gain strength and avoid injury.

The Benefits of Pilates

Muscles can be divided into two groups: prime movers and postural. The prime movers are those muscles involved in movement, such as the hamstrings at the back of the thighs or the deltoids in the shoulders. Postural muscles, such as the deep abdominal muscle called the transverse abdominis, work to maintain stability. This core stability is essential when the body is moving, for example, when creating a firm platform for keeping the pelvis still while running, or controlling the position of the shoulder blade while throwing.

Muscle imbalances can occur through repetitive strain or faulty mechanics, and result in an uneven pull of the muscles around a joint. This imbalance may eventually cause injury to that joint. The pain that results will inhibit the postural or stabilizing muscles around the joint and, as a result, these muscles weaken, making the injured joint even more unstable and still more susceptible to further injury and pain. And so the cycle repeats. Even when the area is no longer painful, these muscles do not automatically strengthen again. This is why injuries tend to reoccur. To recover fully from injury, the muscles in that area need to be specifically strengthened and their co-ordination retrained again.

Trunk or core stability requires strength, endurance and co-ordination of the stabilizing abdominal, pelvic floor and lower back muscles. Stability is necessary to

below The anterior and posterior views of the human muscular system show the main muscles of the front and back of the body. Although this is a simple diagram only, it will help you to gain a clear understanding of the location of the muscles used throughout your Pilates practice. Be aware, though, that Pilates uses many other supporting muscle groups during different phases of a movement.

THE MUSCULAR SYSTEM

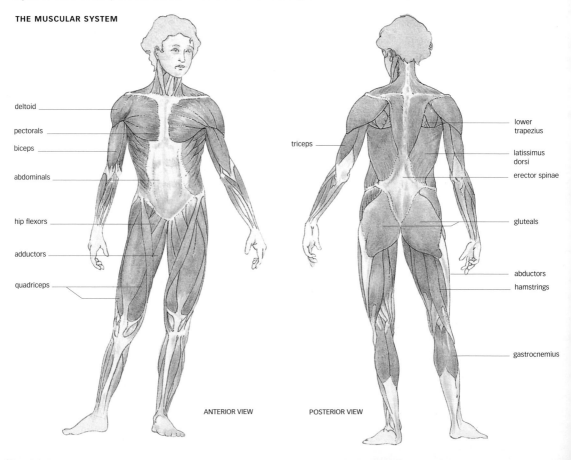

deltoid

pectorals

biceps

abdominals

hip flexors

adductors

quadriceps

triceps

lower trapezius

latissimus dorsi

erector spinae

gluteals

abductors

hamstrings

gastrocnemius

ANTERIOR VIEW

POSTERIOR VIEW

left Throughout the day try to give yourself a posture bodycheck. Try to pinpoint your bad habits as awareness is half the battle.

more energy, extra alertness during waking hours and a general sense of well-being.

For the more experienced exerciser, Pilates can help to highlight imbalances throughout the body. The attention to detail and the concentration given to the movements can challenge even elite professional athletes, who often comment that they feel like beginners again after trying it. What appear to be the simplest of movements can be incredibly challenging when performed correctly, so do not worry if even the first position of an exercise seems hard to you: in terms of Pilates this is a good thing. As long as you work at your own pace, paying attention to how your body feels during the movement, Pilates is perfectly safe and very effective.

support and protect the lower back from injury, to help with general postural alignment and to allow the release of the hips for greater freedom of movement. Better core stability can therefore reduce the chance of injury. Improving it is often the way finally to get rid of niggling back problems that you may have suffered from for years. Core stability exercises are an important part of the Pilates method, which focuses on improving the strength and control of these stabilizing muscles.

The Pilates programme is very enjoyable and you should soon feel results which will motivate you to continue. If you adhere to it, you will be rewarded by improved posture, an enhanced feeling of balance, reduction in aches, pains and stiffness, greater flexibility and a longer, leaner, more toned body. As your posture improves, you will look as if you have lost weight, and one of the most frequently heard comments from people who are new to Pilates is that they feel "as if they have grown". This is because they have learned to lengthen up through the spine to its maximum potential, making them look slimmer and feel more confident.

Regular Pilates sessions will help your co-ordination and enhance your balance, which is of special importance through the

aging process. You will gain strength in a balanced way, so that tight, tense areas are stretched and weak ones strengthened. The realignment of your body will also make it easier for you to use it correctly. You will feel more relaxed and less stressed and will possibly benefit from other "by-products" such as more refreshing sleep,

right Many osteopaths recommend Pilates to aid recovery and rehabilitation as well as a way of preventing possible imbalances or injuries. Remember though, if you feel pain or have an existing injury, always check with a medical professional before starting a new exercise programme.

PILATES AND OSTEOPATHY

My introduction to Pilates followed a serious back injury. I was eager to recover as quickly as possible, and for the injury not to recur. I am a competitive runner (a former International 400m runner), so I did not want the injury to affect my training. I found a class and was impressed by the specificity of the exercises and how much more stable my back felt after several weeks of regular sessions. Since maintaining a regular regime, my back has felt better and my sports performance has improved. I now incorporate clinically based Pilates exercises into the rehabilitation of my patients and recommend it to them as an excellent way to improve their own stability.

Alex Fugallo
DO, ND, Bsc (Hons) Osteopathic Medicine
Registered Osteopath

The Exercise Environment

It is important to "set the stage" for your Pilates routine, creating a serene environment that will not divert you from the mind-body connection. So, before you begin, block out any distractions and ensure that your exercise session will not be interrupted. Here are a few tips for preparing your exercise environment:

• Find a comfortable, quiet area to work in, where you will have enough room to lie down without hitting your head on the coffee table.

• Turn off your phone, the television and any other machines that might disturb your routine.

• Aim to create gentle lighting, using natural daylight if possible or a soft lamp.

• Burning essential oils can help to create the right atmosphere: try lavender if you want a relaxing, calming session or orange to uplift or invigorate. Lemon is refreshing and is said to aid concentration: simply experiment to see what suits you.

• It is important to use a good exercise mat. Look for one that will protect your spine when you lie down; it should be firm but have enough padding so you can't feel the floor. Make sure it is non-slip and long enough for you to lie on when you are completely stretched out.

• Wear comfortable clothes; cotton is best. Avoid tight elastic bands, but do not wear very baggy clothes: you will feel stronger and sleeker in contoured clothes which allow you to move and stretch freely.

• Listen to soft, relaxing music with no harsh sounds. New age or classical music works well. Alternatively, a recording of natural sounds or crashing waves might be a good choice.

• Try not to have a heavy meal before starting exercise of any kind. Digesting the food while you are trying to work your muscles could cause cramps or indigestion. Allow at least two hours after a main meal before exercising. If you are hungry before you exercise eat a piece of fruit to tide you over.

below Create a spacious and comfortable area for practising Pilates. Remove any distractions so that you will not be disturbed and wear comfortable, streamlined clothes so that you feel in tune with your body throughout.

• It is important to be well hydrated at all times – especially when exercising. Always have a bottle of water to hand and take small sips throughout the session. Drink water before and after exercise, and try to get into the habit of always having water with you.

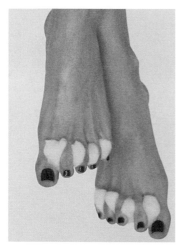

above Pilates is performed barefoot. You could paint your toenails so that you feel beautiful while working out.

above Using gentle lighting helps to set a calm mood especially during the relaxation phases of your workout. Scented candles can be very calming, especially fresh sea scents.

• A sports drink is only necessary if you will be exercising strenuously for 90 minutes or more. Sports drinks replenish lost electrolytes (these are sodium, potassium and chloride) but this is not a problem unless you sweat excessively during an extended bout of exercise.

• Pilates is done barefoot, so do not worry about trainers or socks. This helps you to judge more accurately the distribution of weight in your feet as you exercise.

• Before you start your Pilates session spend a couple of minutes (longer if it is possible) focusing on how your body feels. Do you feel tension in any specific area or are you stiff or tight in certain muscles? Be your own fitness advisor and tailor your routine around your body's needs. For example, if you feel stiff then you may choose to add more stretches into your programme for that day for a better workout.

above Try to drink a little before and after your Pilates session, and take sips whilst you exercise. Water is the best drink. Not only does it keep you hydrated but you will have the added benefit of glowing skin.

• You know your body better than anyone else does. Be aware that your body's needs change daily and try to respond to those needs. Be prepared to adjust your routine in order to gain maximum benefit from your programme. But take care to keep your routine balanced so that you are not just doing the exercises you find easy.

Key Elements of Pilates

Some concepts are referred to repeatedly in Pilates: these are the "key elements" that make it more than just a sequence of movements. Keep them in mind throughout your sessions, relating them to each exercise, and as you become more familiar with the technique they will start to make more sense to you. They will help you to get the most benefit from each movement, and also keep the exercises safe and comfortable. Some of these key elements will come more naturally to you than others, but do not feel discouraged. They will eventually become automatic and you will find yourself applying the same principles to other forms of activity, because they are based on attention to detail and alignment, safety and commonsense.

Breathing

Breathing is something you do unconsciously, but when you are relaxed and calm your breathing pattern is different from when you are tense, anxious or negative.

At times of tension and stress, breathing is usually irregular and shallow, and does not completely fulfil your need for oxygen. If you learn to control your breathing while practising Pilates as well as during daily activity, it will help you to maintain your energy and stay relaxed.

Holding your breath causes tension in your muscles, which decreases when you exhale. For this reason, athletes learn to exhale when executing certain movements such as a tennis serve, a basketball dunk or a golf swing: they are programmed to exhale on the maximum effort. In sports that require a maximum effort during a longer period of time, such as power-lifting, elite athletes will hold their breath. This gives their muscles added stability but has several potentially negative effects on their blood pressure. Remember that these athletes are aiming at a particular goal: they want to win medals at all costs, sometimes even by endangering their health. You should never

hold your breath when exercising. In Pilates, it is sometimes difficult to gauge which of the movements is the one that takes maximum effort. Most of the movements maintain tension in the torso at all times, but your breathing should always be regular and relaxed.

When starting out on this or any other exercise programme, strive to master the general movement first, then focus on the breathing patterns. It is often the case that correct breathing patterns start to come naturally as the body tries to help itself, but you can practise breathing control exercises when you are not moving to help you learn the correct technique. During the exercises try not to let the ribs flare up (push upwards and outwards away from your spine), which sometimes goes hand in hand with arching the spine. Aim to keep the ribs the same distance from your hips, just sliding them out to the sides and then back again as you breathe. This is described as breathing laterally.

Breathing exercise

Here is a simple breath control strategy that you can practise at any time. Regulating your breathing will enhance your body awareness and control and make you feel calm and centred.

1 Place your hands with your palms under your chest, on your ribs, and your fingers loosely interlocked. Inhale slowly and continuously through your nose, to a count of four. Do not strain, keep yourself relaxed.

2 As you inhale concentrate on allowing your ribs to expand laterally: your fingers should gently part. Don't let your ribs jut forward. Exhale slowly, expelling all the breath from your lungs, then repeat.

left During your Pilates session you must give each movement your full concentration. Really focus and feel the muscles working.

right If you do not feel in complete control of a movement, then try a less intense version. Return to the more advanced variation at a later date.

Concentration

Your muscles respond better to a training stimulus if the brain is concentrated on the effort. Remember that it is the brain that sends out the signal to the muscle to contract. So, it is imperative that you concentrate on the work you expect the muscle to perform.

It is very easy to get distracted while exercising if you do not set the right mood, avoiding intrusive sounds or disturbances that will take your mind off what you are doing. It is also necessary to prepare yourself mentally to focus on your body and the work that it will be doing.

Control

All movements should be performed slowly and with absolute control. The faster you do anything, the less actual muscle mass you will use to do the exercise: instead, you will be

below Try to begin and end each session with a few moments of complete relaxation.

using momentum. Most Pilates movements are not static; they should be continuous but at the same time controlled and precise.

Flow

Pilates movements cannot be likened to repetitions of a conventional exercise. They are continuous. Try to "link" one movement with the next, maintaining a steady flow of energy

above Maintain a steady flow of energy, keeping movements graceful and fluid.

throughout the session. You will not be stopping and starting as in conventional exercise, but flowing like a steadily turning wheel.

Relaxation

Pilates is a gradual re-education of the body, and in order to benefit from it you must try not to create unnecessary tension. This would eventually create an imbalance in the body, which is the very thing you are trying to remedy. Watch especially for tension in the neck and jaw, but you may hold it anywhere – even in the feet. During a session, give yourself little mental checks from head to toe and you will start to see where you tend to hold tension. Awareness is half the battle.

Adherence

No exercise programme works unless you do it! Adopt this programme as part of your life and make it as much part of your daily routine as brushing your teeth: physical activity is as much a way of taking care of your body as personal hygiene.

above Pilates practice must be consistent in order for you to see and feel the benefits.

Core Strength

The principal aim of the exercises is to create core strength, which will be the powerhouse for the rest of your body. When you reach a level of understanding of core strength Pilates starts to feel like an altogether different form of exercise: you begin to get a feel for your body working as a whole in a very focused, concentrated way.

The abdominals and back form the centre of the body, from which all movements in Pilates are initiated. If you look at a ferris wheel in a funfair, there is movement around the wheel but the powerhouse is the centre because everything is controlled from there. This is how you should view your body. Your centre should be your first priority, because without sufficient strength in this area you are vulnerable to injury. So, what are these muscles and how do you locate them?

right The illustration displays the key abdominal muscles used in Pilates. These are the muscles used when we refer to "working from a strong centre" or developing "core strength".

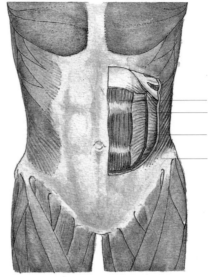

rectus abdominis
transverse abdominis
internal abdominal obliques
external abdominal oblique

Muscles that stabilize the torso

Rectus abdominis: This is a wide and long muscle that runs all the way down from the sternum (breast bone) to the pubic bone. The rectus abdominis helps to maintain correct posture and allows forward flexion.

Obliques: These are located at the waist, and there are actually two sets: the internal and external obliques. They allow you to rotate at the waist as well as flexing laterally (to illustrate this, imagine that you are picking up a suitcase by your side).

Transverse abdominis: This muscle is located behind the rectus abdominis, like a "girdle" wrapped around your stomach. It is used when you draw your navel towards your spine, and is the muscle that contracts when you cough.

Building core strength

By stabilizing the torso you are creating a "co-contraction" between the abdominal muscles and the back muscles. This means that all these muscles are working together to create a stable entity. In most people they are weak, and in the back they can be tense and tight. In this situation the spine may be pulled out of alignment, causing improper posture and risk of injury. When the back muscles and the abdominals are strong and flexible it becomes easier to maintain correct posture. Pilates strengthens and stretches these core muscles, helping to correct imbalances and reducing the chances of suffering back pain.

left Pilates exercises are designed to build up your core strength.

Locating the transverse abdominis

Sit or stand upright, inhale and pull your stomach towards your back, imagining that you are wearing very tight jeans and trying to pull your tummy away from the waistband. This is what you will be doing during all the Pilates exercises.

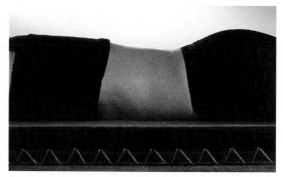

1 Lie on your tummy with your head relaxed and supported on your folded hands or on a small cushion under your forehead. Keep your head in alignment with your back and the back of your neck long, without shortening the front. Try to keep your hip bones on the floor and relax your shoulders.

2 Inhale, then as you exhale pull your navel towards your spine, trying to create an arch under your abdominals. You may not be able to lift very far up at first: this is not important as long as you understand the concept. Gently lift your shoulders back and draw your shoulder blades down your spine.

above If sliding your shoulder blades down your spine is a baffling request, practise this subtle movement by standing up with your arms by your sides. Keeping your back straight, push your fingertips towards the floor. Do not force your arms down or lock them into position. Try to keep the shoulder blades close to the back of the ribcage. This is very useful for limiting tension around the shoulders, which tends to make you pull your shoulders up to your ears.

above Every movement should be controlled via your abdominals. Keep bringing your attention and focus back to pulling your navel towards your spine.

Neutral Spine

A healthy spine has natural curves that should be preserved and respected but not exaggerated. The term "neutral spine" refers to the natural alignment of the spine. If you have any serious pain in your back, check with a physician before embarking on any exercise programme. The main curves are:

1 **The cervical spine**: the area behind the head, along the back of the neck, is concave; it should curve gently inwards.

2 **The thoracic vertebrae**: the largest area of the back curves very slightly outwards.

3 **The lumbar spine**: the lower back should curve slightly inwards; it should not be flat or over curved.

4 **The sacral spine**: the sacral curve is at the bottom of your spine and curves gently outwards.

It is important to allow the spine to rest in its natural position to prevent stresses and imbalances. During Pilates movements you

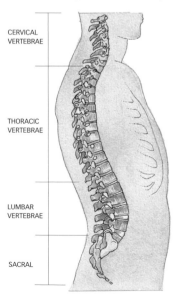

CERVICAL
VERTEBRAE

THORACIC
VERTEBRAE

LUMBAR
VERTEBRAE

SACRAL

Finding neutral spine

The importance of neutral spine cannot be emphasized enough, as it allows your spine to elongate and relax. Before starting an exercise it can be helpful to roll gently between the two extreme positions and then try to fall comfortably between the two.

1 Tilt your pelvis, flattening your back into the floor.

2 Tilt your pelvis in the opposite direction, creating an arch under your lower back. Make this movement slow and take care not to hold for too long or you may cause tension in your lower spine.

3 Find a position between these two extremes in which your back feels natural and comfortable: this is neutral spine. Unless otherwise stated, you should always work from this position during your Pilates routine.

should ensure (unless otherwise directed) that your back is not flat or pushed into the floor, although this can be tempting in order to achieve a flatter tummy. What you tend to do in this position is grip at the hip flexors (the muscles located at the top of the thighs) thus creating tension in a place that is commonly tight anyway. You must also try to avoid over curving your spine, as this pushes the abdominals forwards and tightens the muscles around the spine. "Neutral spine" lies in between these two extremes and echoes the natural and safe position that your spine prefers.

left The diagram shows the four natural spinal curves. These curves help to cushion some of the shock from our daily activities – even walking creates some mild stress. One of the key elements of Pilates is the close attention given to the alignment of the spine during all movements.

Pelvic Floor Muscles

The pelvic floor muscles act as a dynamic platform at the base of the pelvis, functioning both as a support mechanism and as an aid to bowel and bladder function. Well-trained pelvic floor muscles may also improve orgasmic potential in women and erectile function in men.

Pelvic floor muscle activity is a "lift and squeeze" movement: it is the action used to stop midstream urine flow and to stop the passage of wind. It is essential to perform this movement accurately in order to improve the muscles. A woman can tell if she is using the correct muscles by examining herself with a mirror. During a pelvic floor muscle contraction she should see an anal squeeze and an upward movement of her perineum. Inside the vagina, she or her partner should be able to feel a vaginal pressure. A man should see an anal squeeze with the penis lifting at the same time.

Once you have found the correct movement, the next part of the strengthening process is to hold the contraction and to repeat it. At first, you may be able to perform only short holds, but the aim is eventually to hold each contraction for ten seconds. The number of times that you repeat the contraction also depends on your ability; the aim is eventually to repeat the hold ten times.

As well as these sustained holds, you should also practise short, sharp, fast contractions, again in sets of ten. To strengthen the muscles you will need to exercise them up to six times a day. To maintain the resulting change you should remember to exercise them to their full ability at least once a day.

As the brain controls the action of muscles in groups rather than individually, it is important when exercising to consider those muscles that work well together. It is now believed that the pelvic floor muscles work best in conjunction with the transverse abdominis, which is contracted constantly during Pilates exercises. Once you are familiar with Pilates movements you can add pelvic floor muscle lifting and squeezing as you contract your abdominals.

Jeanette Haslam
MPhil, MSCP, SRP

right The pelvic floor muscles are often ignored but are important to exercise. For maximum benefit, especially for women who have had children, the exercises should be performed daily.

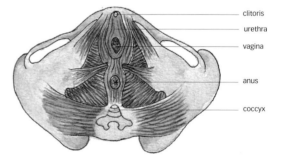

clitoris
urethra
vagina
anus
coccyx

above When you become more familiar with Pilates, try adding pelvic floor contractions as you exercise.

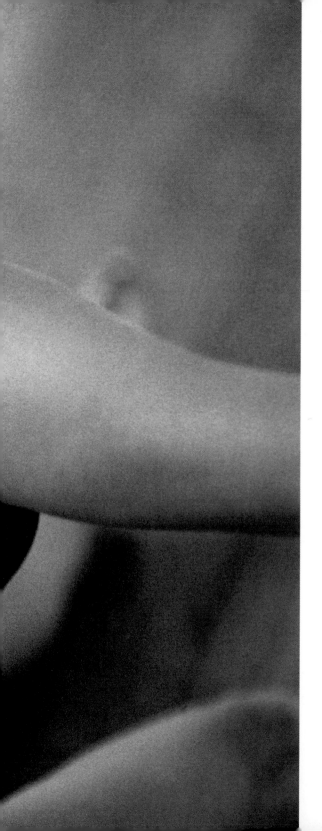

Warming up and Mobility exercises

This chapter is dedicated to preparing the body for the demands we are going to make on it. One of the benefits of warm-up exercises is that fluids are released into the joints, making the muscles more pliable, reducing the risk of injury as well as making muscular responses faster and more precise. By regularly practising mobilizing exercises, you decrease your risk of sustaining injuries when exercising and make even everyday activities easier to perform.

Exercises for Warming Up

The first part of any exercise routine should be a warm-up to raise the core temperature of your muscles. If you pull a cold elastic band too hard it snaps, but once it is warm it becomes more pliable and will stretch further. The same applies to your muscles. The warm-up prepares you psychologically for activity, getting you in the mood. It also increases the efficiency of the neuromuscular pathways, thus speeding up the signals sent from the brain to your muscles.

Keep your movements flowing and gentle during the warm-up: do not force your body or overstretch. Adopt the correct breathing patterns each time and keep the spine in neutral. Repeat each of the warm-up exercises five times.

Perform all exercises with flow and complete concentration. Work from a strong centre and avoid holding on to any unnecessary tension. Breathe wide and full.

Arm crosses

These are great for warming up the shoulders and upper back. The movement should be continuous and flowing: think of the graceful way in which a ballet dancer's arms move. As you do the exercise, watch for tension in the neck; your spine should stay in neutral and your abdominals hollowed. Imagine you are trying to reach both sides of the room and lengthen out through your arms and up through your spine.

1 Stand with your feet about hip-width apart and cross one hand in front of the other. Relax your shoulders and lengthen up through your spine, keeping your head in alignment.

2 Inhale to prepare and, as you exhale, take your arms out to the sides, palms up. Keep your shoulders relaxed and slide your shoulder blades down your spine as you lift your arms. Lower your arms to begin again. This should be performed at a moderately fast pace but should always be controlled and flowing.

Shoulder circles

A good way to relieve tension in the shoulders and upper back, this exercise also mobilizes the shoulders. It is a movement that many people tend to stumble on naturally when they are feeling stiff. Make the movement slow and controlled, breathing in wide and full through the ribs. Keep the spine in neutral.

1 Stand with your feet hip-width apart, lengthen up through your spine and do not let the abdominals sag. Inhale to prepare. As you exhale, roll your shoulders forwards up to your ears and then around.

2 Concentrate on trying to form a complete circle. Think about the shape you are making: is it a circle or an egg-shape? Create as big a circle as you can in one direction then the other.

Arm sweeps

This big, sweeping movement will wake you up and help with a "fuzzy head". It also mobilizes the spine, lower body and shoulders. Try to move in a fluid, rhythmic way at a constant speed.

1 Stand with your feet close together, knees and shoulders relaxed, keep the abdominals hollowed. Extend your arms overhead and lengthen up through the spine while keeping your feet flat on the floor and your head in alignment.

2 Inhale to prepare, then drop your chin to your chest and roll down through your spine, letting your arms flow behind you.

3 Bend your knees as your arms sweep back and again as you bring them forward and up over your head to begin again, lengthening up through your spine as you return to standing.

Walking through the feet

You may be surprised at how stiff your feet and ankles get, and this exercise is designed to wake up the feet, ankles and calves. It's a good idea to warn them gently of the activity to come, so that they provide a strong, secure base.

left From standing, lift the heel on one foot then the other in a natural walking movement, bending the knees. Keep the spine in neutral and the abdominals hollowed. Keep this movement rhythmic and continuous, always lengthening up through the spine.

Standing balance

This is a more advanced way to warm up the feet and lower legs, which may also challenge your balance. Try to keep your weight central and concentrate on each part of your foot as you rise and come back down on to your heels. This movement is performed at a moderately slow pace.

left Stand with your feet hip-width apart and make sure that your toes are not clenched but relaxed. Keep your spine in neutral, abdominals hollowed, and place your hands on your hips to help you balance. Keeping your head in alignment, come all the way up on to your toes. Hold the balance for a few seconds, then lower your heels slowly to begin again.

Relaxation position

This is not a movement, just a comfortable position. Try always to start and end your Pilates sessions with a couple of minutes in the relaxation position. It will help you focus and get in contact with your body, as well as making you feel relaxed and refreshed. Concentrate on each area of your body, from your head down, and try to observe any tension, particularly in your jaw and face, shoulders and hips. Some people even clench their feet. Just notice where your areas of tension are and gently focus on relaxing. Try to visualize your spine lengthening and sinking into the floor. Imagine you are lying on warm sand and let it support your spine. This position can also be used at any time during the day, whenever you get a chance to relax.

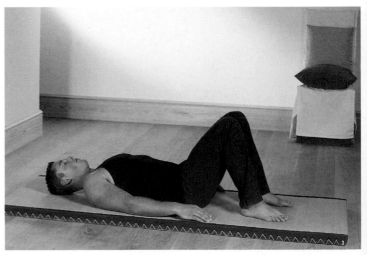

above Lie on your back with your knees bent and your feet flat on the floor. Your spine should be in neutral. Relax your shoulders and let your shoulder blades gently glide down your spine, but do not force them into position. Your head should be in alignment with your spine and your arms relaxed by your sides. Breathe wide and full laterally, in through your nose and out through your mouth.

Exercises for Mobility

During the aging process, our range of movements can decrease making everyday activities harder, increasing our risk of injuries. The following exercises guide you safely and effectively through a series of exercises that challenge mobility, so helping to keep the joints healthy and flexible. Some of the exercises also challenge your co-ordination, balance and strength.

Rolling down the spine

Now you are ready to start your Pilates session with some mobilizing exercises. This is a really effective movement for mobilizing the spine, and can be very refreshing if you have a stiff back. However, if you have problems with your spine take advice before doing it. If you find it difficult you can do it with bent knees or against the wall, and you can also keep your hands on your thighs. Keep the movement flowing and remember not to collapse into it: the abdominals should not sag. During a Pilates programme, you can use this as a transitional movement to transfer from a standing to a floor exercise, so that the feeling of flow is not lost.

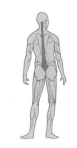

Purpose: To mobilize the spine and improve balance
Target muscles: Designed to loosen/mobilize the spine
Repetitions: Repeat 6 times

Checkpoints
• Create space between each vertebra
• Bend your knees and keep your hands on your thighs if required
• Create a C-shaped spine

2 As you bend over from the hips, create a C-shape with the spine, letting the arms hang towards the floor. Feel your head relax and your shoulders drop. Don't sway backwards or forwards as you roll down. Make the movement flowing and controlled.

3 Start to curl back up, tilting the pelvis and trying to mobilize each part of the spine, uncurling it bone by bone and creating as much length as possible between the vertebrae. Try not to lean backwards or forwards but keep your weight in alignment, with your feet flat on the floor. As you come up to standing feel the crown of your head float up to the ceiling.

1 Stand with your feet hip-width apart, balancing your weight evenly through your feet. Breathe in to begin and, as you exhale, lower your chin to your chest, and start to roll down towards the floor.

One leg circles

Circling the legs mobilises the hip joints and also challenges core strength, as you aim to keep the hips still during movement of the lower body, your thighs get a workout too. Keep the abdominals hollowed throughout. Make sure your spine stays in neutral and your shoulder blades glide down your back. The ribs may move away from the hips in this position so keep gently reminding yourself to control them. Make the circles flow and keep the movement continuous: think of a ballet dancer's grace and poise.

FIRST POSITION

1 Lie on your back with your knees bent and your arms by your sides. Keep your spine neutral, your head aligned and the supporting foot firmly on the floor, raise one bent leg. Ensure your hips are square and still. Then start to circle your knee. Make small circles initially then larger ones, using your abdominals for control. The breathing for this movement requires concentration: break each circle into semicircles, inhaling as your leg crosses your inner thigh and exhaling on the outer edge of the circle.

Purpose: To mobilize the hips and build core stability
Target muscles: Adductors, hip flexors and abdominals
Repetitions: Circle 5 times in each direction, then change legs and repeat

Checkpoints
• Keep the hips square: don't let them lift from the mat
• Keep the spine in neutral
• Make the circle as large as you can safely control

SECOND POSITION

2 Straighten the moving leg, keeping the other foot firmly on the floor. Lengthen up through your toes and try to make your leg as long as possible. If your hips start to move, you are not controlling the movement and would be better off continuing to work with a bent leg. Try to increase the size of the circle as you get stronger.

Checkpoints
• Keep the abdominals hollowed throughout the movement
• Extend the circle as you grow stronger

THIRD POSITION

3 Straighten the supporting leg and lengthen, as if you were trying to reach the end of the room. Continue to lengthen up through the circling leg. Make the circles only as large as you can control. This position is really tough, so do not try to progress to it until you feel you have complete control in the second position. Remember to work from a strong centre.

Checkpoints
• Guard against over-curving of the spine
• Lengthen through both legs

The shoulder bridge

A very popular exercise in almost every class, this is a good mobilizer with which to start your session and a wonderful way to ease a stiff back. After this exercise your spine should feel loose and supple and it will also work your abdominals and lower body. The aim is for each bone in your spine to lift off the mat in succession. You may find that, to begin with, your back lifts in two or three sections: try to create length between each vertebra. As you lower yourself, place each vertebra in turn on the mat, imagining a pearl necklace sinking on to a velvet cloth.

The hips should be perfectly level, and you should try to create as much distance between your hips and your shoulders as possible. Do not forget to tilt the pelvis as you begin the movement. To mobilize the spine fully be sure to return to neutral as you lower your back to the floor, just before you tilt the pelvis and start the next lift.

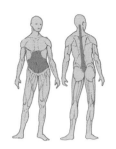

Purpose: To mobilize the spine and challenge the abdominals
Target muscles: Erector spinae, abdominals
Repetitions: Repeat 6 times

Checkpoints
- Keep the hips level
- Maintain the distance between the hips and the ribs
- Make the movement flow

1 Lie on your back with your arms by your sides, slide your shoulder blades down your spine and lengthen your arms away. Bend your knees and place your feet hip-width apart flat on the mat. Your head is in alignment and your spine in neutral.

2 Tilt your pelvis and lengthen the tailbone away. The whole length of your spine should be in contact with the mat.

3 Slowly peel your spine up off the mat bone by bone, raising your hips towards the ceiling and keeping the abdominals flat and drawn down. In this position it is common to flare the ribs, so concentrate on keeping a constant distance between the hips and ribs. Make the movement smooth and flowing, inhaling as you lift and exhaling as you come down. Once you get used to the movement you can increase the stretch by taking your arms over your head.

Abdominal
and Back
exercises

The following exercises concentrate mainly on the abdominals and back – the staples of Pilates – although of course the body works as a unit throughout every movement. Feel the abdominals getting stronger, flatter and firmer as you progress and watch your wardrobe change. Your back will respond by allowing you to live your life in comfort, free from the burden of aches and stiffness. Pay attention to the alignment of your body throughout the day, for optimum results.

Rolling Back

Once you have mastered this movement, it is bound to bring back memories of childhood. We all rolled back and forth when younger and it did wonders for our backs. But do remember that it may not be as effortless now that your back has stiffened up – and make sure you work on a mat that gives plenty of support. Once you have practised rolling down the spine with your hands on the floor, try progressing on to rolling back: you may not roll back up on your first attempt, but keep practising. When pulling in the abdominals, imagine you are squeezing a sponge held between your navel and your spine. Squeeze the sponge as hard as you can. Take care not to roll back on to your neck.

Purpose: To mobilize and massage the back and strengthen the abdominals
Target muscles: Erector spinae, abdominals
Repetitions: Repeat 6 times

Checkpoints
• Keep your feet flat on the floor
• Lengthen up through the spine at the end of the movement
• Tilt the pelvis

FIRST POSITION

1 Sit with your spine in neutral and your knees bent with both feet flat on the floor. Place your hands near your hips with your fingers facing your feet. Inhaling wide and full through the ribs, draw your navel towards your spine. Lower your chin towards your chest then, using your hands for support, start to roll down to the floor. Try to place each vertebra on the floor, one by one. To do this, tilt your pelvis and curve your spine into a C-shape.

2 Once you have rolled down as far as you find comfortable, exhale and, using your core strength, return to the starting position. Pull up through the crown of your head to create a long spine, then repeat. Use your arms only as support and avoid transferring all your weight onto your triceps.

SECOND POSITION

1 Sit upright with your spine in neutral. Lengthen up through the spine and imagine your head floating up to the ceiling. Place your feet flat on the floor and your hands just below your knees. Don't overgrip: keep your elbows bent and your chest open. Take care not to tense or grip around your neck.

2 Inhale as you tilt the pelvis and curve the spine into a C-shape to roll back, tucking in your chin and keeping your thighs close to your chest. As you exhale, use your abdominals to pull you back up to the starting position. Try not to use momentum, but make the movement flow at a consistent speed. Between each roll lengthen up through the spine.

Checkpoints
• Keep the chin tucked into the chest
• Do not grip the neck
• Use your abdominals to get you back to the starting position again

The Roll-up

In spite of the name of this exercise, you begin by rolling down. It is an excellent way to strengthen the abdominals but is very challenging, so ensure you are comfortable and confident with the first position before moving on. Although you are curving your spine do not collapse into the movement. Roll down only a little way at first to get the feel of the movement, then roll lower as you become stronger. At all times, do a mental check that you are not tensing other parts of your body, such as your neck or face. As you come back to an upright position imagine that you are sitting against a cold steel door.

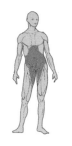

Purpose: To strengthen the abdominals
Target muscles: Abdominals, hip flexors
Repetitions: Repeat 10 times

Checkpoints
• Do not overgrip the legs, use them only as support
• Lengthen up through the spine in the starting position
• Feel the abdominals pull you up

FIRST POSITION

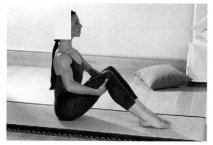

1 Sit upright with your feet flat on the floor and your knees bent. Hold the back of your thighs, with your elbows bent and your arms open; don't overgrip. Your spine should be in neutral. Lengthen up through the spine but do not grip the neck. Slide the shoulder blades down the spine.

2 Inhale and tilt your pelvis to create a C-shaped spine. Keeping your feet flat on the floor, roll down bone by bone, creating space between the vertebrae. Your hands are there to support you if you lose control but try to rely on abdominal strength to stabilize the movement. As you curl down, imagine your spine is a bicycle chain that you are placing down link by link. When you have lowered down as far as you can, exhale and contract the abdominals to roll back up to the starting position. Sit upright, keeping the spine in neutral.

SECOND POSITION

1 This time, hold your arms directly in front of you, level with your shoulders. Your elbows should be bent, arms rounded. Let your shoulder blades glide down your spine and feel the crown of your head "float" up towards the ceiling. Inhale and tilt your pelvis to begin the downward roll as before.

2 When you first progress to this position try a few small roll-downs to get the feel of the movement before going down further. Feel the support of the abdominals throughout the downward and upward roll. Keep your feet flat on the floor all the time.

Checkpoints
• Use the abdominals, not momentum, to pull you up
• Lower bone by bone
• Do not collapse into the movement
• Keep the feet on the floor

The Hundred

This static contraction builds core strength and is one of the most commonly taught Pilates exercises. Challenge yourself to reach a hundred.

The Hundred really tests your co-ordination. Try not to stagger your breathing as you count your taps:

the breath should be flowing and even. Pay special attention to any tensing in the neck and face in this position. To help you do this exercise well, visualize a heavy weight balancing on your abdominals and pulling your navel down towards your spine.

FIRST POSITION

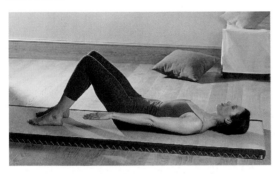

1 Lie on your back with your knees bent, your feet flat and your head in alignment. The spine should be in neutral and the abdominals hollowed, drawing the navel to the spine. Your arms are by your sides, lifted off the mat. Slide your shoulder blades down your spine. Inhale as you count to five then exhale for five. Gently tap your fingertips on the floor and co-ordinate your breathing with your taps. Breathe steadily and laterally into your ribs.

Purpose: To strengthen core muscles, co-ordinate breathing patterns and build endurance.
Target muscles: Transverse abdominis, rectus abdominis, stabilizing mid-back muscles
Repetitions: 20 x 5 beats

Checkpoints
• Keep your arms lengthened
• Draw the shoulder blades down the spine
• Keep the abdominals hollowed

SECOND POSITION

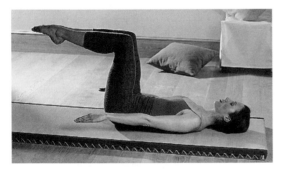

2 When you feel confident about the first position, lift your feet off the floor. Your knees should be directly above your hips and your feet level with your knees. Do not allow your knees to fall away as this will cause your spine to curve. If this is too much of a challenge you can raise just one leg, but do not twist your hips. Repeat the breathing pattern as before. Keep the abdominals flat throughout and maintain the distance between your hips and ribs.

Checkpoints
• Glide your shoulder blades down your spine
• Keep your knees above your hips
• Toes are pointed
• Feet stay level with knees

THIRD POSITION

3 Curl your upper body off the floor, dropping your chin towards your chest so that you are facing your thighs. Do not grip your neck and keep drawing your shoulder blades down your spine. Maintain the breathing pattern for a hundred beats as before. If you want a greater challenge, try straightening the legs. Lower your eyes in this position to check that your abdominals are flat and your ribs are not flaring up.

Checkpoints
• Release tension from the neck
• Do not clench your jaw
• Keep the abdominals flat

The Swimming

This exercise is a favourite with physiotherapists as it is a very effective way of developing strength in the core muscles. It is a very challenging exercise but is an easy one to cheat on, so read the instructions carefully to make sure that you are performing the exercise correctly. Ensure that you keep your abdominals lifted. Instead of just raising your arms and legs, visualize them lengthening away from your trunk. Do not try to lift them too high from the floor. Make your movements elegant and flowing and avoid throwing your arms and legs or collapsing back onto the floor on the way down. Take care not to lift your hips off the floor or to overbalance onto one side or the other.

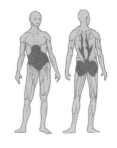

FIRST POSITION

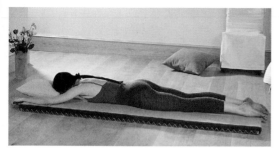

1 Lie on your front, placing a small pillow under your forehead to keep your head in alignment with your spine, which is in the neutral position. Keep your neck long. Stretch your arms over your head and lengthen them away. Point your toes and lengthen your legs away. Breathe laterally, wide and full. Draw in your abdominals, imagining that there is a drawing pin on the mat that you are lifting away from.

Purpose: A strength exercise, challenging co-ordination and core strength
Target muscles: Abdominals, gluteals, erector spinae
Repetitions: Repeat 10 times

Checkpoints
• Do not tip your head back
• Keep the abdominals lifted
• Breathe laterally

SECOND POSITION

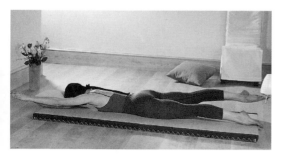

2 Introduce a challenge to your core strength by lifting one leg. Exhale as you lift and inhale as you lower the leg. Keep both hips in contact with the floor, and do not try to lift the leg too high. Keep lengthening as you lift, maintaining the distance between the ribs and hips. Do not lose the lift in your abdominals. Take care not to twist the raised leg but keep your knee and foot in line with your hips. Repeat with the other leg.

Checkpoints:
• Lengthen as you lift the leg
• Do not twist the hips

THIRD POSITION

3 As you exhale, lift your opposite arm and leg together. When you lift your arm raise your head and upper body with the movement, but keep facing the floor so that your head stays in line with your spine. Lengthen through your arms and legs and keep your hips in contact with the floor. Remember the drawing pin under your navel: if you lose the lift in your abdominals, continue to work in the second position for a while longer.

Checkpoints
• Keep your head in line with your spine
• Do not twist the torso
• Lengthen from a strong centre

One Leg Stretch

Do not be fooled into thinking that this is a relaxing leg stretch – it is actually a very challenging movement which builds core strength and is also good for improving co-ordination. Keep your hips still throughout as if they were being held in a vice. Take care not to curve your spine and keep your shoulder blades pulled down your spine and close to the back of your ribs throughout. If you find the hand position difficult, you can lightly hold either side of your knee instead. Make sure that you are just making light contact and do not over grip as this causes tension in the neck and jaw. Your upper body should be stabilized by your abdominal muscles.

Purpose: To strengthen abdominals and improve co-ordination
Target muscles: Abdominals, stabilizing back muscles
Repetitions: Repeat 10 times on each leg

Checkpoints
• Hollow your tummy throughout
• Keep the hips still

FIRST POSITION

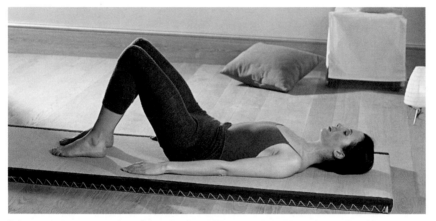

1 Lie on your back with your knees bent and your feet flat on the floor. Your spine should be in neutral and your head in alignment: do not shorten your neck by tipping your head back or dropping your chin to your chest. Draw the navel to the spine.

2 Lift one foot off the floor, keeping the knee bent, and pull the leg gently towards you, supporting it at the knee. Try not to overgrip, causing tension in the neck, and keep your foot in line with your knee. Take care not to let the ribs flare up. Repeat with the other leg, inhaling as you lift and exhaling as you lower.

SECOND POSITION

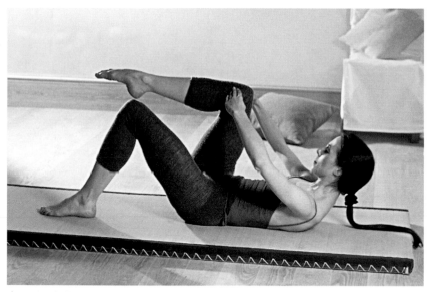

Checkpoints
- Do not tip the head forward or back
- Watch for tension in the neck

above When the first position is understood, curl the upper body off the floor and continue the same movement. Let the chin fall towards the chest, and try to limit tension in the neck. Keep the hips very still, controlling any movement from the hips via your abdominals. Breathe laterally. Keep the stomach hollowed throughout the movement, trying to make it as flat as possible.

THIRD POSITION

Checkpoints
- Pull the shoulder blades down your spine close to the back of your ribs
- Lengthen the legs away
- The lower your straight leg, the harder your abdominals have to work

above This position really challenges your co-ordination. As you raise the right leg, place the right hand on the ankle and the left hand on the inside of the knee. Change hands as you change legs. As one leg comes in to the body the other leg lifts and lengthens away on an exhalation. Keep your toes pointed and stretch down through the straight leg. The movement is controlled by the abdominals: keep them hollowed, and maintain the distance between the ribs and hips. Do not twist the hips: imagine they are being held in a vice. Keep the pace slow and consistent.

Leg Pull Prone

This is actually a yoga position as well as a modified Pilates position. You will gain a lot of torso strength and stability from this exercise, and if you do it properly it will feel as if every muscle in your body is being challenged. Remember to breathe freely throughout the exercise and do not hold your breath when holding the position. It is common to shrink down into your shoulders in this position so try to maintain the length in your neck throughout. Keep checking for tension around the neck, face and shoulders. Focus on your abdominals which should be stabilizing your whole body. You could try to visualize a drawing pin inserted through your navel and attaching to your back.

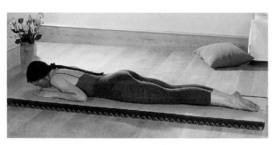

Purpose: To strengthen the abdominals and spine and challenge the upper body
Target muscles: Abdominals, stabilizing back muscles
Repetitions: Repeat up to 10 times

FIRST POSITION

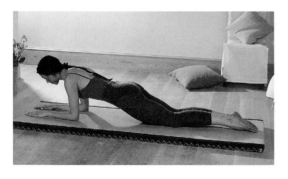

1 Lie on your front with your head in line with your spine. Bend your arms and keep your upper arms close to your body. Lift the abdominals off the floor, imagining that you are creating an arch under your stomach. Breathe wide and full. Focus on this abdominal lift and aim to hold it for one minute before relaxing again.

Checkpoints
- Slide your shoulders down your spine
- Keep the upper arms close to your body

SECOND POSITION

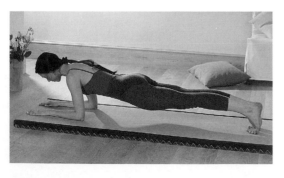

2 Your elbows should be directly under your shoulders. Do not push your buttocks towards the ceiling or arch your spine. Keep your head in line with the spine and lengthen it away: don't sink into your shoulders or squeeze the shoulder blades together. Make sure that your hips stay square. The abdominals are lifted throughout. If this is too difficult, lower your hips and curl just your upper body off the floor. Try to hold this for one minute.

Checkpoints
- Maintain a straight line from your head to your knees
- Do not let the abdominals sag

THIRD POSITION

3 Lift up on to your toes, straightening your legs. This is a real challenge, so be sure to have worked on the first and second positions for quite some time before progressing. Take care not to transfer all the weight into your shoulders or upper body, and keep your hips square. Pull your navel to your spine, maintaining the distance between ribs and hips, and breathe laterally. Aim to hold for up to one minute.

Checkpoints
- Keep a straight line from your head to your heels
- Do not transfer all your weight into your upper body
- Draw your shoulder blades down your spine

The Side-kick

This is another good exercise for core strength, concentrating on the lower body. Have patience and work gradually through the progressions to achieve the best results.

When performing the Side-kick take care not to use momentum to lift and lower your leg. It may help to visualize moving your leg through mud as this will slow you down.

Your foot or knee should stay in line with your hip throughout the movement. Be aware of the alignment of your hips and keep them stacked on top of one another as it is common for the hips to roll forwards and the posture to collapse. This movement is stabilized by the abdominals and the obliques (the muscles at the side of the waist). Try to keep a constant connection with their involvement.

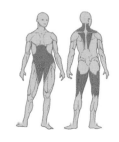

Purpose: To challenge core strength and work the lower body
Target muscles: Hamstrings, hip flexors, abdominals, stabilizing shoulder muscles, abductors
Repetitions: Repeat 10 times each side

FIRST POSITION

1 Lie on your side, resting your head on your outstretched lower arm. Keep your head in line with your spine, which is in neutral, and your hips stacked vertically: they must not roll in or out. Your knees are bent, one on top of the other. Place your free hand in front for balance but do not lean into the supporting arm or transfer your weight forward.

2 Lift the top knee directly above the other knee. Inhale and, with your toes pointed, move the knee back as you exhale until it travels behind your body. The challenge is to keep your hips stacked and your abdominals hollowed. Your shoulder blades should be pulled down your spine and your ribs should not be pushed up. You should feel this in your side. To increase the challenge, straighten the top leg, keeping the toe pointed.

Checkpoints
• Do not transfer all your weight into the arm in front
• Keep your abdominals flat

SECOND POSITION

above Straighten both legs. This is very challenging so be sure to advance only after working with the previous position first. Bring the bottom leg forward slightly from your hip, it should not be in line with your spine. Keep the hips vertical and lengthen out through both legs. The control comes from your centre. Exhale as the leg travels backwards.

Checkpoints
• Do not let the hips collapse
• Lengthen out through the legs

The Side-squeeze

This exercise will shape the waist and abdominals, so it is especially good for the area that hangs over your waistband when you wear fitted clothes. As you lift, check for tension in your neck or other parts of your body, and watch that your ribs stay down. Do not let the abdominals sag but hold them taut throughout.

If you wish to add an extra challenge, raise the top knee, keeping it in line with your hips – no higher. Make this a slow, controlled movement. Take care not to overgrip with your hands. Perform the movement with flow, avoiding any jerky movements when lifting and lowering.

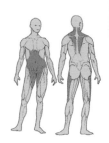

Purpose: To strengthen the waist and mid-section, stabilizing and improving balance.
Target muscles: Obliques, shoulder stabilizers, abdominals and abductors
Repetitions: Repeat 10 times on each side

Checkpoints
• Do not allow the abdominals to sag
• Keep your hips stacked
• Maintain the distance between your ribs and hips
• Really feel the muscles in your side working

1 Lie on your side with your knees bent and in line with your hips. Your hips are stacked and your abdominals hollowed. Place your hands on your head, directly opposite each other. Do not tip your head back or drop your chin to your chest. Breathe in.

2 Exhale as you lift your upper body off the floor and inhale as you lower. Make the lift slow and controlled. Don't jerk your neck or grip too hard with your hands. Maintain the length through your spine and take care not to let your hips collapse, but keep them stacked. Make sure your knees stay level with your hips. Draw your shoulder blades down your spine.

The Side Bend

This movement may look simple but it creates a marked improvement around the waistline if you practise it regularly, as well as developing core stability and balance. Feel the movement being controlled by your torso.

Take care in this position not to let the hips roll either inwards or outwards. Imagine that you have a red dot on your hips that should always face the ceiling as you lift. Maintain the length in your neck and avoid sinking into your shoulders. You may not be able to lift very far off the floor initially but do not worry as the real benefit comes from maintaining the correct alignment and performing the exercise accurately. You might find that this exercise is less challenging on one side than the other: it is common for one side to be a little stronger.

Purpose: To strengthen the abdominals and sides and improve balance
Target muscles: Obliques, abdominals, stabilizing shoulder muscles and latissimus dorsi
Repetitions: Repeat up to 10 times on each side

FIRST POSITION

1 Lie on your side with your legs bent, knees level with hips and feet in line with knees. Imagine there is a rod running vertically through your hips. Rest on your elbow, which should be directly under your shoulder, and bring the other arm in front for support. Resist the temptation to push all your weight on to the supporting hand or the resting elbow

2 Inhale, breathing laterally, and as you exhale lift your hips off the floor. Use the muscles in the side closest to the floor to initiate the movement and control it via a strong centre. Hollow the abdominals, drawing navel to spine, slide your shoulder blades down your spine and ensure that your ribs are not pushing up.

Checkpoints
• Initiate the movement via a strong centre
• Do not transfer all your weight on to your arms
• Keep the neck soft

SECOND POSITION

Checkpoints
• Make sure the hips do not collapse
• Keep the abdominals hollowed
• Lift straight up, not veering to either side
• Keep the movement flowing

above Progress only after reaching a level of ease in the first position. If you feel ready, straighten your legs and lengthen them away. Cross one foot over the other, with the toes pointed, to support you as you lift your hips. Keep your head in line with your spine and lengthen up through the top of your head.

Upper and Lower Body

exercises

Although Pilates is a holistic form of exercise, these movements concentrate particularly on upper and lower body strength. A number of repetitions is recommended for each exercise, but work at your own pace: if you can perform a movement accurately only twice, do so, increasing the repetitions as you grow stronger. Work your way through the progressions gradually – don't try to do too much too soon.

Push Ups

This is a classic exercise for shaping the upper body: the shoulders and biceps. If it is performed properly your abdominals will get a workout too. Once you progress beyond the first position, if your previous exercise was a standing one you can preserve the flow of movement and loosen up the spine by using a transitional move to get to the floor: follow the instructions for the mobilizing exercise called "Rolling Down the Spine" and, once your hands are hovering at floor level, bend at the knees, place your hands on the floor and move into the starting position for push-ups.

In every position, pull the abdominals in, never allowing them to sag, and keep your spine in neutral. Check for tension in your neck. Build up gradually to the full push-up.

Purpose: To strengthen the upper body
Target muscles: Deltoids, pectorals, biceps, stabilizing back muscles and abdominals
Repetitions: Repeat up to 10 times

Checkpoints
• Keep your head in line
• Do not allow the abdominals to sag

FIRST POSITION

◀ **1** Stand facing a wall and place your hands on it. Your hands should be level with and just wider than your chest and flat against the wall, with the fingers pointing upwards. Your feet stay flat on the floor. Keep your spine in neutral and lengthen up your body, feeling your head "float" towards the ceiling.

◀ **2** Bend at the elbows to bring your chest towards the wall. Keep your head in line with your body, slide your shoulder blades down your spine, and check that you are not pushing up your ribs. Push away from the wall to come back to your starting position. Keep the movement slow and controlled.

SECOND POSITION

Checkpoints
• Do not lock the elbows
• Lower only as far as you can control
• Keep your chest at hand level and your head forward of your hands

1 Position yourself on all fours, knees directly under your hips and hands directly under your shoulders, with the fingertips facing forwards. Keep your spine in neutral and don't let your head sink into your neck.

2 Keeping your head in line with your spine, exhale as you lower your chest to the floor between your hands by bending your elbows. Do not allow the abdominals to sag. As you push up, straighten the arms without locking the elbows.

THIRD POSITION

Checkpoints
- Keep a straight line from your head to your knees
- Do not let your buttocks stick up
- Do not arch or curve your back

▲1 Drop your hips so that there is a straight line from your head to your knees. Your fingertips should be facing forwards and hands directly under the shoulders. Keep the abdominals strong and your hips square.

▶ 2 Exhale as you lower and inhale as you lift. Keep your head in line with your spine and forward of your hands. Don't let your ribs flare up. Keep your weight evenly distributed between your knees and your hands.

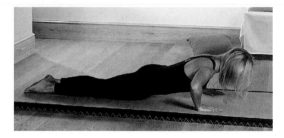

FOURTH POSITION

Checkpoints
- Keep your shoulder blades down the spine
- Make it a controlled, flowing movement
- Breathe laterally

▲1 Form a straight line from your head to your feet, supporting yourself on your toes and hands. The fingertips should face forwards and your head should be in alignment with your spine.

◀ 2 Lower your chest to the floor between your hands, then push up, keeping your elbows soft. Keep the movement controlled and continuous. Lower only as far as you can control.

Tricep Push Ups

A common complaint is the lack of muscle tone at the back of the upper arm: this is excellent for challenging this area. It works by adapting the classic push-up to work on the triceps. The movements may look the same but there are subtle – but very important – differences. The elbows stay close to the body this time. To help you keep your elbows into your sides, visualize doing the movement in a narrow space between two walls. Try to maintain a constant, and slow, speed throughout the exercise, although this can be very difficult to maintain on the last few repetitions.

FIRST POSITION

▶ **1** Stand facing a wall. Place your hands flat against the wall, fingers pointing upwards. Your hands should be level with and just wider than your chest. Your feet stay flat on the floor. Keep your spine in neutral and slide your shoulder blades down.

▶ **2** Bend at the elbows to bring your chest towards the wall as you exhale. Unlike the classic push up your elbows should remain close to the body and pointing down at all times. Keep your head in line with your body and check that you are not pushing up your ribs. Push away from the wall to come back to your starting position.

Purpose: To strengthen the upper body and the abdominals
Target muscles: Triceps, pectorals, deltoids and abdominals
Repetitions: Repeat up to 10 times

Checkpoints
• Do not let your elbows "wing" out to the sides
• Watch for your shoulders moving up towards your ears
• Lengthen up through the top of your head

SECOND POSITION

1 Position yourself on all fours, with your hands directly under your shoulders, fingertips facing forwards. Keep your spine in neutral and maintain a straight line from your head to your hips. Don't let the abdomen sag.

2 Exhale as you lower your chest to the floor. This time, bend at the elbow and ensure that your elbows point towards your feet, with your upper arms staying close to your sides. As you push up, straighten the arms without locking the elbows.

Checkpoints
• Keep your chest level with your hands
• Keep your head forward of your hands
• Keep your feet flat on the floor

THIRD POSITION

1 Drop your hips so that there is a straight line from your knees to your head. Glide your shoulder blades down your spine. Your fingertips should face forwards.

Checkpoints
- Do not let your buttocks stick up
- Feel the movement in the back of your upper arms
- Do not rely on momentum

2 Exhale as you lower and inhale as you lift. Keep your head in line with your spine. Ensure that your head stays the same distance from your hands and that the elbows are pointing in the direction of your feet. Try to perform the exercise with flowing, continuous movements.

FOURTH POSITION

Checkpoints
- You should really feel this in the triceps
- Keep your body in alignment
- Hollow the abdominals
- Maintain a straight line from your head to your feet

above Make sure you have been practising the modified positions for some time before progressing to this position. This time your whole body should be in one straight line. Don't let your head sink into your shoulders. Lower the chest to the floor, keeping your elbows pointing towards your feet and using the same breathing pattern as for the previous positions.

upper and lower body exercises

Tricep Dips

This exercise is indispensable for firming up the muscles at the back of the arms. The tricep runs from the shoulder to the elbow and can be hard to work, but if neglected, this is the part of your arm that wobbles when you wave. Before you begin, find a chair that offers support at the correct height and check that it will not slip away from you. Work through the full range of the movement by straightening the arms, but take care not to "lock out" the elbows. Lengthen up through the top of your head.

Purpose: To tone the triceps
Target muscles: Triceps, abdominals
Repetitions: Start gently but work up to 20 times

Checkpoints
- Keep your back close to the chair
- Do not lock your elbows
- Keep your head in line

FIRST POSITION

1 Place yourself in front of the chair with bent knees and feet flat on the floor. Support yourself on your hands with your fingers pointing forwards. Lengthen up through your spine, which is in neutral. This is your starting position. Make sure that your abdominals are hollowed throughout the exercise.

2 Bend your elbows and lower your body as you inhale. Glide your shoulder blades gently down your spine and watch that your ribs do not push up. As you return to the starting position on an exhalation, take care not to "lock out" your arms, just straighten them. Keep your back close to the chair and make sure your elbows travel backwards rather than out to the sides. Execute the movement with control.

SECOND POSITION

left Start in the same basic position as above, but this time put your legs straight out in front of you with your toes pointed. Keep your back close to the chair, your elbows pointing straight behind you and fingers pointing down. In this advanced position it is very tempting to let the elbows travel out to the sides, particularly if you are tired, or not paying full attention. Ensure that your head does not sink into your shoulders and remember to breathe fully. Your breathing should be wide and full allowing your ribs to expand fully, but your abdominals should be hollowed out throughout. Aim to keep the movement flowing and continuous, and don't let the pace speed up or down. In this way you will work the muscle harder and get the most benefit from the exercise.

Checkpoints
- Do not use momentum
- Keep the abdominals hollowed
- Maintain an even flow

Exercises for Thighs

The following exercises pay attention to the inner thighs and hips. Although you will be predominantly toning the lower body, you should still focus on hollowing out the abdominals. Ankle weights can be added to both of these exercises. Alignment is very important for these exercises so follow the directions carefully, letting the movements flow rather than "throwing" the leg.

The outer thigh blaster

If practised regularly, this exercise will really firm up the outsides of the hips and thighs and strengthen the lower body. Do not let the abdominals sag, and slide your shoulder blades gently down your spine. Maintain a constant distance between your ribs and your hips and keep the hips square, moving only your leg. Watch for tension elsewhere in the body as you do the exercise.

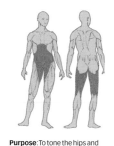

◀ **1** Stand facing the wall with your hands at chest level and flat against the wall. Bend one leg at the knee so that your foot is level with your knee and both knees are in line. Your spine should be in neutral and your foot flexed. Check that there is a straight line from your head to your feet, resisting the temptation to lean into the wall or bend at the hip.

◀ **2** From this starting position, take your knee out to the side. It is important to keep your foot flexed and your knees aligned. Exhale as your leg travels away from your body, inhale as you bring it back. You should not swing the leg. Don't "sink" into the supporting leg, but keep lengthening up through the spine.

Purpose: To tone the hips and lower body

Target muscles: Abductors, abdominals, adductors and hamstrings

Repetitions: Repeat 10 times with each leg

Checkpoints
- Keep your lifted foot in line with your knee
- Keep the rest of your body still; only move the working leg

The inner thigh lift

This is a popular exercise that is often done badly. However, when it is performed correctly it works wonders with that much complained about area, the inner thigh. To progress the exercise you could use ankle weights, but you should really get a feel for the inner thigh initiating the movement before moving on.

1 Lie on your side, supporting your head on your outstretched arm. Your hips should be stacked and your other hand can rest in front of you on the floor for support. Bend the top leg and rest your knee on the floor. Straighten the lower leg and lengthen it away on the floor with the foot flexed. Do not curve your back or allow your ribs to jut forwards. Glide your shoulder blades down your spine.

2 Inhale and, as you exhale, lift the bottom leg as high as you can, keeping the abdominals hollowed all the time, then lower it. Make the movement flow, trying to avoid any jerky movements or, worst of all, swinging your leg. You should feel the muscle of the inner thigh doing the work. Take care not to twist the knee. Keep your foot in line with your leg: there is a tendency to lead with the toes in this position.

Purpose: To tone the inner thigh

Target muscles: Adductors and abdominals

Repetitions: Repeat 10 times on each leg

Checkpoints
- Do not roll hips
- Do not curve the spine

The Open V

This is not one of the most graceful-looking movements, but it works wonders for the thighs, especially the inner thighs, and also benefits the abdominals. It is very important to pay special attention to keeping your knees (and feet in the second and third positions) directly above your hips at all times. If your feet fall towards the floor, your lower back may curve upwards which could cause stress. Check that you are not holding any tension in the shoulders or neck. To create an extra challenge try placing a cushion between your knees. Of course, you won't be able to open your legs so far.

Purpose: To firm up the inner thighs
Target muscles: Adductors, hip flexors, abdominals and stabilizing back muscles
Repetitions: Repeat 10 times

Checkpoints
- Check that your feet do not drop down
- Keep your feet flexed
- Do not curve your spine

FIRST POSITION

1 Lie on your back, with your knees bent and directly above your hips, and your feet level with your knees. Your feet should be flexed. Your arms are on the floor, lengthening away, your shoulder blades slide down your spine, and your head is in alignment with your spine. Start with your knees apart.

2 Keeping your feet in line with your knees, bring your knees together and squeeze to feel your inner thighs working. Hold for a few seconds, then return to the starting position. Keep your abdominals hollowed throughout and your spine in neutral.

SECOND POSITION

Checkpoints
- Do not allow your legs to drop away from your body
- Do not let the legs open too far
- Squeeze the knees together

1 The basic movement is the same as before, but is done with straight legs. Lengthen up through your heels and keep your feet flexed. Start with your legs apart.

2 Bring your legs together and squeeze to work your inner thighs. Keep the hips still via the abdominals, which are hollowed throughout. Keep your arms strong, and really feel your inner thighs working.

THIRD POSITION

Checkpoints
- Watch for tension in the neck
- Lengthen the arms away
- Lengthen up through the heels
- Slide your shoulder blades down your spine

above Curl your upper body off the floor, watching for tension in the neck and shoulders. Don't let your head sink into your shoulders, but glide your shoulder blades down your spine. Watch that your ribs do not flare up. Keep hollowing the abdominals: you can glance down and check that they are held flat. Squeeze the legs together as before.

Cleaning the Floor

This movement will improve your balance and strengthen your lower body and all the small muscles in your feet and ankles – it is great for weak ankles. Initially, you may find the balance quite challenging. If so, it may help to look at a fixed point on the wall. It is common to find that your balance is better on one side than the other as most people favour one side. One of the objectives of this exercise is to balance any subtle differences in strength. Concentrate on maintaining the alignment between your foot and knees. If it helps, imagine that your supporting leg is held between two narrow walls.

Purpose: To strengthen lower body, feet and ankles
Target muscles: Quadriceps, supporting muscles around feet and ankles, abdominals
Repetitions: Repeat up to 10 times on each leg

Checkpoints
• Watch for your knees rolling inwards or outwards
• Keep your supporting foot flat on the floor
• Lengthen up through the spine
• Make the movement smooth and continuous

FIRST POSITION

◀ **1** Stand up tall and imagine the crown of your head floating up to the ceiling. Feel your spine lengthening. It should stay in neutral throughout. Keep your abdominals as flat as possible. Place your hands on your hips and keep your head in line with your spine. Keeping your knees in line with one another, let one foot hover above the floor as you balance evenly on the other.

◀ **2** Bend the supporting leg and lower your body as far as you can control. Do not collapse into the movement. The supporting foot may feel a little wobbly at first. Check that the knee of the supporting leg stays in alignment with the foot. Inhale as you come back up to standing. Keep your upper body strong and watch that your ribs do not travel away from your hips.

SECOND POSITION

left Bend your knee and lower as far as you can into the position as before. This time, you are going to hold this position and then very carefully lower your chest towards the floor. Bend only a little initially. To get back to the starting position, straighten your torso first then come back up to standing. Keep your head in line.

Checkpoints
• Do not try to lower too far
• Do not collapse into the movement
• Keep lifting the abdominals

One Leg Kick

This core exercise really challenges your co-ordination as you cannot see the movement – you just feel it. It is fantastic for toning up the lower body while challenging core strength. A good way to visualize the movement is to imagine that you are squeezing a pillow between your hamstrings and your calf. Try to resist just placing the leg: really feel the hamstrings working. This is a deceptively hard movement so do not worry if it takes practice. You may find it easier to get a feel for the movement first, then add the correct breathing pattern and work on lengthening down through the other leg.

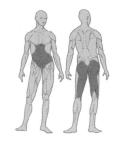

FIRST POSITION

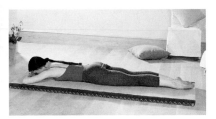

1 Lie on your front, supporting your forehead on your folded hands to keep your head in alignment. Draw your navel to your spine, trying to form an arch under your abdominals.

2 Relax the neck. Avoid clenching the jaw. Relax your shoulders and slide the shoulder blades down your spine. Bend one leg at the knee. This is your starting position.

Purpose: To tone lower body and develop core stability and strength

Target muscles: Hamstrings, erector spinae (when upper body is lifted), abdominals, gluteals

Repetitions: Repeat 10 times with each leg

Checkpoints
- Keep the movement swift and continuous
- Limit any movement by keeping the abdominals hollowed throughout
- Slide the shoulder blades down your spine

3 Inhale and, as you exhale, point your toes and make a stabbing movement with your foot towards your buttocks. Keep your knees together and lengthen through the legs.

4 Ease out of this position then repeat, this time with your foot flexed. Then extend your leg back to its original position. Meanwhile, the supporting leg on the floor should be lengthening away at all times.

SECOND POSITION

left Perform the same movements, but this time curl your upper body off the floor and rest on your elbows. Slide the shoulder blades down. Keep your neck long throughout and watch that your ribs do not travel away from your hips. Lengthen through the spine. If you feel a pinch in your spine in this position, stay with the first position for a while.

Checkpoints
- Keep your neck in line throughout the exercise
- Breathe wide and full
- Do not push all your weight into your arms

Stretches

Throughout your Pilates sessions you will be stretching and lengthening, but here is a whole chapter to take you by the hand through one of the most popular parts of most classes – the stretches. Notice how your range of movement will re-adjust, giving you more freedom and mobility in your daily tasks. Stretching is also linked to a reduced risk of injury – something everyone can appreciate. Many people notice a distinct "lift" in their mood after stretching, feeling refreshed and invigorated, with a general sense of well-being.

Spine Stretch

If your back feels tight or if you just want a healthy and mobile spine then this is the stretch for you. You will feel longer, stretched and more flexible. This is a flowing movement, not a static stretch. To keep your spine lengthening up and to stop you collapsing into the stretch, imagine that you have a beach ball in front of you, and lift up and over the ball. As you come upright again, imagine that your back is rolling up a pole, vertebra by vertebra, and take care to keep this alignment from your head to your hips: do not lean forwards or away from the imaginary pole.

Purpose: To stretch the spine

Target muscles: Erector spinae, hamstrings, adductors and abdominals

Repetitions: Repeat 10 times

FIRST POSITION

1 Sit upright with your knees bent and your feet flat on the floor. Create as much length through your spine as possible. Keep the shoulders relaxed.

2 Let your chin gently drop to your chest, then roll down bone by bone through your spine. As you do so, gently reach forwards with your hands. Keep your abdominals hollowed throughout. Roll back up to the starting position and lengthen up through your spine. Do not collapse into the stretch, but lift up through the abdominals and spine. Exhale as you lower into the stretch.

Checkpoints

• Do not collapse into the stretch

• Keep the movement flowing and continuous

• Let your head float up to the ceiling

SECOND POSITION

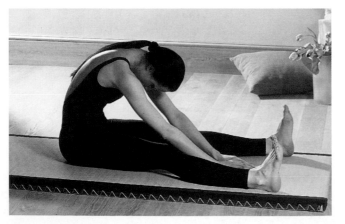

left The movement is the same as before, but this time straighten the legs and flex your feet, lengthening the heels away. Bend the knees slightly if you find this uncomfortable. The legs should be parted as far as is comfortable. As you roll up create as much length as possible between the vertebrae. Keep your buttocks on the floor.

Checkpoints

• Do not have the legs too far apart

• Visualize reaching up and over a beach ball

• Roll up vertebra by vertebra

Spine Twist

A deceptively challenging movement, this twist will stretch the waist and lower back while strengthening the abdominals. To gain the maximum benefit, it is important to keep your bottom on the floor throughout this movement. Let your head float up to the ceiling and pull your navel towards your spine. Try to keep the movement smooth and continuous. On your first attempts at this exercise you may be surprised how hard it is to sit correctly aligned. We all develop certain postural habits and this exercise challenges them so it will feel intense at first. It gets easier with practice.

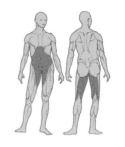

FIRST POSITION

1 Sit upright, lengthening up through the spine, with your knees bent and feet flat on the floor, legs slightly apart. Cross your arms loosely across your chest. Maintain a straight line from your head to your bottom.

2 Breathing laterally, inhale and, as you exhale, turn the upper body to one side, keeping your buttocks firmly on the floor. Repeat on the other side. Remember that this is a flowing movement, not a static position.

Purpose: To stretch the sides, strengthen the abdominals and promote thoracic mobility
Target muscles: Obliques, abdominals, adductors and hamstrings
Repetitions: Repeat 10 times on each side

Checkpoints
• Keep the movement flowing
• Hollow the abdominals
• Lengthen up through the spine

SECOND POSITION

left The basic movement is the same but is performed with straight arms, lengthening out through the arms from the shoulders. Take care not to drop them. Now you are stretching in two directions: lengthening out through your arms and up through your spine. Slide your shoulder blades gently down your back and keep your feet flat on the floor.

Checkpoints
• Do not collapse into the movement
• Keep the whole of your buttocks on the floor
• Do not curve the spine

THIRD POSITION

left The movement is the same but this time straighten the legs and point your toes. You are now stretching in three directions: up through your spine, out through your arms and through your legs. Be sure to keep your buttocks on the floor. You may be tempted to lean into one side as you turn.

Checkpoints
• Lengthen all the way to the toes
• Feel the abdominals working

Lower Back Stretch

This is a good warm-up stretch. Taking deep breaths can help you to relax into the stretch and you may find your muscles becoming more pliable, allowing you to ease yourself further into the movement. The stretch is great for easing mild tension in the lower back, which is a common complaint. Some people find it beneficial to rock slightly from side to side while in this stretch as this can gently mobilize the lower back. To do this, keep your upper body on the floor and make the movement very subtle. Although a number of repetitions are recommended, these are only a guideline until you are confident about your instincts. Hold the stretch for longer or repeat if you need to.

Purpose: To stretch the lower back

Target muscles: Erector spinae and gluteals

Repetitions: Stretch twice; hold for 30 seconds each

Checkpoints

• Check for tension in the neck and shoulders
• Relax into the stretch
• Do not overgrip with your hands

FIRST POSITION

left Lie on your back and bring both knees up towards your chest. Support your legs with your hands, just below your knees. Relax your shoulders and feel the stretch in your lower back. Remember to keep your abdominals hollowed. Inhale to prepare and exhale as you lift your legs.

SECOND POSITION

left Curl your head and shoulders off the floor, imagining curling up like a ball. Keep your neck soft: do not force your head forwards to your knees. Take care not to overgrip – keep your elbows open.

Checkpoints

• Curl up and down slowly
• Make sure your mat is thick enough to protect your back

Spine Press

This movement mobilizes and stretches the lower spine. It is a good one to try whenever your lower back feels stiff, especially if you have been sitting for a long period, at your desk for example (and it can be done very discreetly). The curve of the spine should be very subtle. Take care not to over curve your spine as you may "pinch" the muscles in the lower back. If it feels uncomfortable to curve your spine, or you have problems with your lower back, you may want to perform the second part of the movement only. When you tilt your pelvis, initiate the movement by imagining you are pressing your navel towards your spine. Avoid collapsing into the movement by lengthening your spine.

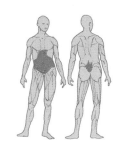

Purpose: To mobilize and stretch the lower back
Target muscles: Erector spinae and abdominals
Repetitions: Stretch twice; hold for 30 seconds each

Checkpoints

- Do not overcurve your spine
- Keep the abdominals hollowed
- Keep your head in alignment

1 Stand a short distance away from the wall, with your back against it, your knees bent and your arms by your sides. Lengthen up and glide your shoulder blades down your **spine**.

2 Inhale and, as you exhale, push your spine flat against the wall by tilting your pelvis and contracting your abdominals. Keep your head in alignment. Try not to collapse into the movement: keep your abdominals hollowed.

Simple Stretches

The following stretches are great for lengthening fatigued, tense muscles. The two upper body stretches are great for opening up the chest; this is ideal if you have been sitting at a desk for a long period of time. On the first Chest Stretch, the wrist is also being slightly stretched. If this is uncomfortable, turn your hand round so that your fingertips point to the ceiling. In the Deep Chest and Back Stretch, slightly bend your knees if your legs are stretched beyond the comfort zone. When performing the gluteals stretch, be sure to keep your bottom on the floor or you will not stretch enough.

Chest stretch

This feel-good stretch is great for relieving tightness in the chest and uses the wall for support. It can be done almost anywhere to relieve tightness in the chest.

Purpose: To stretch the chest
Target muscles: Pectorals
Repetitions: Stretch twice; hold for 30 seconds each

Checkpoints
• Keep your spine in neutral
• Feel the stretch in your chest
• Relax your shoulders

1 Stand sideways to a wall. Extend one arm and place your hand flat on it. Keep your hand in line with your chest and your feet in line with your hips. Draw in your abdominals; your spine stays in neutral.

2 Now turn your hips away from the wall, so that you feel a stretch in your chest. Relax your shoulders and enjoy the stretch. Change sides and repeat the movement.

Gluteals stretch

This stretch is reasonably easy to do and promotes a greater range of movement in the lower body. It is also a valuable stretch to do before many different sports that involve a lot of lower body work.

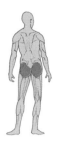

1 Sit on the floor and position one leg in front of the other (the legs are not crossed). Relax your arms in front of you. Lengthen up through the spine, creating space between the vertebrae. Don't worry if your knees don't fall to the floor, just relax and let the knees fall into a natural position.

2 Drop your chin towards your chest and curl down the spine while pushing the arms forwards and keeping your buttocks on the floor. Curl up again, switch the positions of the legs and repeat on the other side. Do not collapse into the movement; keep the abdominals pulled in throughout.

Purpose: To stretch the lower body
Target muscles: Gluteals
Repetitions: Stretch twice; hold for 30 seconds each

Checkpoints
• Keep your buttocks on the floor
• Replace the spine bone by bone
• Create length between the vertebrae

Deep chest and back stretch

This stretch is ideal for easing tightness in the chest and back. Try to relax your shoulders and neck into the stretch. Remember, if this stretch is too intense, you can bend your knees.

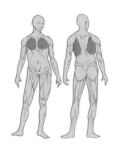

1 Stand facing the wall with your feet together and place your hands flat on the wall level with your shoulders, just wider than shoulder-width apart. Lengthen up through the spine.

2 Inhale, then as you exhale lower your chest by bending from the hips, to feel a stretch in your chest and back. Keep your head in line with your spine. Keep the spine lengthened and the abdominals hollowed.

Purpose: To stretch the chest and shoulders
Target muscles: Pectorals and latissimus dorsi
Repetitions: Stretch twice; hold for 30 seconds each

Checkpoints
• Keep your head in line with your spine
• Keep your hips over your knees
• Bend the knees if necessary

Abdominal stretch

This is a very popular stretch that is similar to the "cobra" in yoga. It is very good for stretching the abdominals after all the hard work they have done. Take care not to throw your head back in this stretch. Keep facing the floor and lengthen up through the top of your head to avoid sinking into the shoulders. If you feel any pinching in your lower back ease gently out of the stretch.

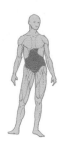

1 Drop your hips so that there is a straight line from your knees to your head. Glide the shoulder blades down your spine. Your fingertips should face forwards.

Purpose: To stretch the abdominals
Target muscles: Abdominals
Repetitions: Stretch twice; hold for 30 seconds each

Checkpoints
• Do not overcurve your spine
• Keep your head in line with your spine
• Keep your hips on the floor

2 Inhale and, as you exhale, lift your upper body off the floor, resting the weight on your arms. Keep the abdominals hollowed and lifted, and take care not to overcurve the spine. Keep your hips on the floor. Do not sink into your neck, but lengthen up through your spine. Watch for tension in the neck. If you feel a pinch in your lower back ease out of the stretch.

Hip flexor stretch

The hip flexors tend to be one of the tightest muscle groups, and when these muscles get overly tight they can cause discomfort and eventually imbalances. People involved in most sports benefit from this stretch, especially runners.

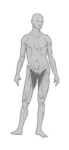

1 Kneel down on the floor and take one step forwards, using your hands for support. If you need extra cushioning, place a pillow under the supporting knee.

2 Lunge carefully into the front leg, exhaling as you lunge forwards. Make sure your raised knee is directly over your foot. Lengthen up through the spine and keep the abdominals hollowed. You should feel this stretch at the top of the rear leg. Change legs and repeat.

Purpose: To stretch the hip flexors
Target muscles: Hip flexors
Repetitions: Stretch twice; hold for 30 seconds each

Checkpoints
• Take care not to collapse into the stretch
• Lunge into the stretch
• Keep your head in alignment

Waist lifts

This is a good movement to stretch and mobilize the spine. If it feels too intense or uncomfortable to have your arms overhead, then stretch with them by your side.

1 Lie on your back with your arms overhead or, if this is difficult, by your sides. Lengthen through your feet, spine and arms: visualize two cars pulling you in different directions. Draw the navel in to the spine.

2 Carefully lift your waist. This is a very subtle movement; take care not to create a big curve in your spine. Keep the abdominals strong and the head in alignment. Watch for any gripping in your lower back. If you feel any pinching in your back, ease out of the stretch.

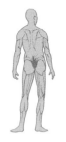

Purpose: To stretch and mobilize the spine
Target muscles: Erector spinae
Repetitions: Stretch twice; hold for 30 seconds each

Checkpoints
• Ease out of the stretch if any pinching occurs
• Keep the abdominals strong
• Lengthen out the spine

Side stretch

This feels good at any time. No wonder cats and dogs are always stretching – it relieves the body of unwanted tension and liberates the spine and joints.

left Sit on the floor with one leg in front of the other (the legs are not crossed). Inhale as you prepare. Exhale as you raise one arm and lengthen up through the spine, then stretch into one side from a strong centre, taking care not to collapse into the stretch. Feel the stretch in your back. Pull the navel to the spine and keep your buttocks on the floor. If this leg positioning is uncomfortable, bend your legs and keep your feet flat on the floor.

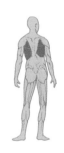

Purpose: To stretch the back
Target muscles: The latissimus dorsi
Repetitions: Stretch twice on each side; hold for 30 seconds each

Checkpoints
• keep your buttocks on the floor
• Lengthen up through the spine
• Don't let the abdominals sag

making
Pilates
a part of your
Life

To be effective, any exercise needs to be organized into a programme that is easy to remember and that you will want to do regularly. This chapter offers you guidance on devising a successful Pilates programme that will help you achieve your goals, and shows you how Pilates can become integrated into your daily life. Keep your programme balanced. Combine it with cardiovascular work and good nutrition to give you a total fitness plan.

Designing a Programme

With Pilates, it can be difficult to identify the muscles that are being challenged as most movements involve a combination of several muscle groups all working together. A Pilates exercise may be overtly working the arms or the legs but at the same time it may be demanding a constant stabilization process from the torso. So you will find that even though a movement is targeting a certain muscle group, you will often feel it in other parts of your body as well.

In general, Pilates movements can be divided into three main categories:

1 **Strengthening exercises** that concentrate on making certain muscle groups stronger and more toned.
2 **Flexibility exercises** that improve the range of motion around a joint.
3 **Mobility exercises** that train the body to move more easily.

left Flexibility exercises will increase your range of movements and help to prevent sports injuries.

Classifying the movements

The exercises described in this book are grouped according to both the action that is being reinforced and the dominant muscles that are being used. For ease of reference, the following lists repeat this classification to help you choose a selection of movements from each group to make up a well-rounded programme. If you find an exercise listed under more than one heading it is because it involves a combination of various actions.

Exercise groups

Exercises that strengthen the upper body
- Push ups (deltoids, pectorals, biceps, abdominals and stabilizing back muscles)*
- Triceps push-ups (triceps, deltoids, abdominals and pectoral muscles)
- Leg pull prone (abdominals, stabilizing back muscles)*
- Triceps dips (triceps, abdominals)

Exercises that strengthen the lower body
- Cleaning the floor (quadriceps, supporting muscles of the feet and ankles, abdominals)
- The shoulder bridge (buttocks and abdominals)*
- The open V (adductors, abdominals, hip flexors and stabilizing back muscles)
- The outer thigh blaster (abductors, abdominals, adductors and hamstrings)
- One leg kick (hamstrings, abdominals, lower gluteals and erector spinae)*
- The inner thigh lift (adductors, abdominals)

Core exercises have been marked with an asterisk (*).

Exercises that strengthen the abdominals and back
- One leg stretch (abdominals and stabilizing back muscles)*
- The side kick (hamstrings, hip flexors, abdominals, abductors and stabilizing back muscles)*
- Leg pull, prone (abdominals and stabilizing back muscles)*
- The roll-up (abdominals, and hip flexors)*
- The side bend (obliques, abdominals, stabilizing back muscles; stretches the latissimus dorsi)*
- One leg circles (adductors, abdominals, and hip flexors)*
- The side squeeze (internal and external obliques, abdominals, shoulder stabilizers and abductors)
- The hundred (abdominals and stabilizing mid-back muscles)*
- Swimming (abdominals, gluteals and erector spinae)*

Exercises that promote flexibility
- Gluteals stretch (gluteals)
- Chest stretch (pectorals)
- Side stretch (latissimus dorsi)
- Hip flexor stretch (hip flexors)
- Spine twist (obliques, adductors and hamstrings; promotes thoracic mobility)*
- Abdominal stretch (abdominals)
- Spine stretch (erector spinae, hamstrings, adductors)*
- Deep chest and shoulder stretch (pectorals and latissimus dorsi)
- Lower back stretch (erector spinae and gluteals)
- Spine press (erector spinae)

Exercises that promote mobility
- The shoulder bridge (spine)*
- Rolling back (spine)*
- Spine twist (spine)* and Spine press (spine)
- Spine stretch (spine)*
- One leg circles (hips)*
- Rolling down the spine (spine)*

above Consistency is one of the key elements in creating and maintaining a strong, healthy physique. Regular Pilates sessions, combined with cardiovascular exercise and healthy eating habits, will ensure positive results.

Core exercises

There is an adaptation process involved in this as in any other exercise programme. This means that your body will need a few sessions to get used to the movements. You will therefore get the best results if you choose a few "core" exercises – movements that are considered pure Pilates exercises – and concentrate on these for a period of time, say four to six weeks, giving your muscles a chance to adapt to the work that is being asked of them. Start with these, and once you feel that you have mastered them (not necessarily advancing to a higher level, just feeling comfortable and confident about the movement), add on a few more.

As you add exercises, try to keep a balance between the main muscles being used: choose one from each group in turn until you have tried them all.

Planning your exercise programme

How much time do you need to dedicate to your Pilates programme? How can you design a programme that will be well-rounded and complete, as well as motivating and enjoyable? When should you change the programme? What if you don't always have time to do it all? To answer these questions you need to take several factors into account.

left You can loosen and liberate your body with the regular practice of Pilates.

1 The time factor

In a perfect world, you would dedicate at least one hour to your Pilates programme and 30–40 minutes to a cardiovascular work-out, and you would do both activities three times a week. However, on those days when there is no time for a complete training session, a short, 25-minute workout is better than none at all.

2 Desired results

Are you trying to win a sporting event or do you just want to get a little fitter? Dramatic results require dedication, time and effort. But an hour of Pilates three times or even twice a week, as well as a weekly minimum of three cardiovascular workouts of 30–60 minutes duration, will raise your fitness level, giving you very acceptable results in a relatively short time.

3 Daily life

Do you have an active job? Do you live at the top of several flights of stairs? Do you drive everywhere or walk? The things that you do when you are not working out also count: your body does not care whether you are in a gym lifting weights or carrying a heavy box to the attic. Obviously, the more sedentary your daily life, the more conscientiously you will have to carry out your fitness plan.

Sample Programmes

The majority of the exercises need to be repeated approximately ten times each (or, in the case of unilateral exercises, ten times per side). Apart from some exceptions – the Hundred is performed for one hundred taps on the mat and the Plank is held for 60–90 seconds – when putting together a programme you can safely estimate that each movement will take about five minutes. A certain group of muscles may need more attention because of, for example, muscular imbalances or repetition of a certain activity. You also need to take into account the initial warm-up, final stretch and a short relaxation period at the end. As an example to get you started, two basic plans are suggested here.

Vary your programme from time to time so that you do not get bored. If you dislike an exercise or it does not feel right on a particular day, do a different movement that targets the same muscle groups. Always listen to your body. Most of the exercises have variations, so work your way progressively through the different levels of intensity.

The short programme

What if you don't have time for a session lasting a whole hour? You can plan a mini programme lasting 25 minutes to do on those days when you just cannot find more time. However, do try to base most of your sessions around the hour-long plan and use the short plan only when you really have to. Twenty-five minutes is not ideal, but it's better than skipping the session entirely. Obviously, you will have to shorten the length of time spent on each exercise, as well as doing fewer of them: aim to achieve five to seven repetitions of each movement.

1

◀ **Warm-up**
8-10 minutes
(p64)

2

◀ **Push-ups**
3 minutes
(p84)

3

◀ **Swimming**
3 minutes
(p75)

4

◀ **Rolling back**
3 minutes
(p72)

5

◀ **Spine stretch**
3 minutes
(p96)

6

◀ **The Hundred**
3 minutes
(p74)

7

◀ **Relaxation**
2 minutes
(p66)

The one-hour programme

In this sample format, the exercises chosen include some of the "core" movements; this would be a good programme to start with while you are learning and adapting to these exercises. As with most Pilates programmes, the emphasis is on the strengthening of the torso.

After a few weeks, you can change some of these movements for others; try always to do some movements from each of the different categories so that you are working on all parts of the body and developing strength, flexibility and mobility.

◀ **Warm-up**
8-10 minutes
(p64)

◀ **The shoulder bridge**
5 minutes
(p69)

◀ **Swimming**
5 minutes
(p75)

◀ **Side squeeze; right side**
5 minutes
(p80)

Side squeeze:

◀ **Side squeeze: left side**
5 minutes
(p80)

◀ **The hundred**
5 minutes
(p74)

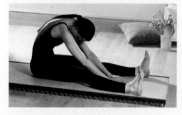

◀ **Spine stretch**
5 minutes
(p96)

◀ **Push-ups**
5 minutes
(p84)

◀ **Rolling back**
5 minutes
(p72)

◀ **The roll-up**
5 minutes
(p73)

◀ **Relaxation**
5 minutes
(p66)

Assessing Common Postural Faults

The human body is a fantastic machine. It is designed to walk, run, jump, push and pull. It is autonomous and multifunctional and can adapt to many different situations - for instance, by strengthening or lengthening its muscles or adding a layer of fat to protect it from the cold. Unless you were born with a particular physical challenge, your body began life as a symmetrical and co-ordinated unit.

Unfortunately, in adult life many bodies are no longer aligned or symmetrical. The two sides function differently, with some muscles overworked and tight while others are weak and overstretched. So what does a perfectly balanced body look like? First, both sides of the body have equal strength and flexibility. The shoulders, hips and ankle joints are level and symmetrical and the shoulder blades are back and down.

Posture check

Stand in front of a full-length mirror and look at your reflection. Just relax and take up your usual stance without thinking about your posture. Assess your stance honestly – or ask a trusted friend for their assessment. Here are some common misalignments of the body. Do you recognize any of these?:

• The head may be tilted to one side, jut forward or tilt backwards.
• The legs may sway backwards.
• There may be a curved "C" shape in the spine.
• The back may be over arched.
• The shoulders are not level or parallel: one may be rotated forward or elevated or both shoulders may be rounded.
• The palms of the hands are turned backwards

• The hip joints are uneven, tilted backwards or forwards or to one side
• The knees and ankles may be rolling inwards or outwards and are asymmetrical
• The feet turn in or out
• The weight is not evenly distributed between the feet
• The arches in the feet are collapsed

There are many reasons why your body has become misaligned. When any part of the body becomes dysfunctional the whole unit is affected. Even though some muscles are not doing their job effectively, you still have to get on with your day-to-day life so other muscles compensate for weaknesses. Using your body in a faulty manner reinforces these imbalances. Eventually you may start to ache in those areas that need to compensate. Aches and pains are the body's

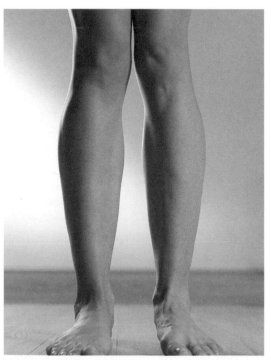

above The knees or ankles may roll inwards or outwards, or may be asymmetrical.

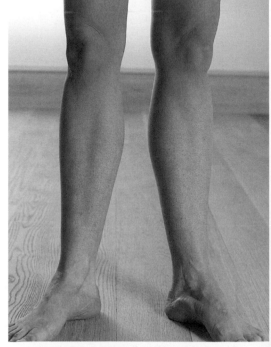

above The feet may be turned inwards or outwards.

left The hip joints may be uneven, with the weight unevenly distributed between the feet.

right The head may be tilted to one side, creating muscular imbalances in the neck and back.

way of alerting you to a problem. You may even get injured or at best suffer chronic pain, commonly in the neck, back, knees, hips or shoulders. It is advisable to get an accurate assessment of the imbalance from a trained professional whilst it is still in its early stages as it is best to try to remedy the problem before your body overcompensates.

Think about the way you feel when you sit for long periods of time. Is your neck sore on one side? Does your lower back ache? This is not the way you are supposed to feel. If your body is doing its job correctly, you should not be experiencing pain or discomfort at any one place in your back or neck from sitting or standing for long periods.

So why are our bodies not doing what they were originally intended for? Most people live in a stress-filled environment. Life has become faster, more is expected, and in order to cope many devices have been designed for increased convenience and reduced effort. Devices like remote controls, lifts and cars have meant that we are less physically active than previous generations.

This lack of activity has led to a rise in obesity levels and conditions such as heart disease. We can no longer rely on general activity to keep us healthy, so we have to look at increasing our exercise levels. Stress and tension in the body can be very damaging, causing imbalances that make muscles over-tight and this can lead to movement becoming restricted.

You can tell a lot about your body from your shoes. Look at a pair of your own shoes with leather (not rubber) soles. Are they more worn on the inside or the outside? Does the sole of one shoe look older than the other? Are the toes pushing against one side of only one of the shoes? Most people have slightly misaligned feet but, if this is a distinct pattern or causes discomfort, it may be worth checking with a qualified specialist. You may have an actual postural deviation that inhibits the maintenance of correct posture. If so, this should be dealt with by a medical practitioner.

right The head may jut forward out of alignment with the spine.

Improving Your Posture with Pilates

The body must be re-educated to cope with the stresses of daily life. In cases where the postural fault is severe, or there is pain, you should see a specialist before attempting this or any other exercise programme. Pilates is not meant to be an alternative to the prescription of a medical professional, but it can be a useful tool to accompany the recommendations of a specialist.

Commonly when people train in a gym they tend to choose exercises randomly, concentrating on the areas of the body they like the least, or doing exercises that they find easy to do: this can reinforce existing misalignments. Unless the body is trained as a whole, as in Pilates, its weaknesses will only be reinforced. The regular practice of Pilates strengthens and stretches all the core postural muscles, making correct posture far less of a muscular effort and more of an unconscious act.

To understand the whole picture it is essential to realize the importance of the torso. Every step you take, every weight you lift and every movement you make must be stabilized by the muscles of the abdominals and the back to protect the spinal cord against injuries. It does not matter how strong your arms are, unless your torso can protect you by stabilizing internally, your strength will be limited. Think of your body as a chain of muscles: you are only as strong as your weakest link.

If your posture is not good, your muscles will have been working in an incorrect manner for a long time. You cannot force them into place in a few sessions; there will be a period of adaptation. Always seek medical advice if you feel pain either during or after exercise. However, it is good to learn to differentiate between sore muscles and pain. Muscle soreness is par for the course

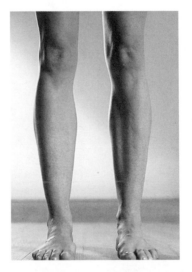

right When you are standing in the correct manner, the knee and ankle joints are symmetrical and the knees face forwards.

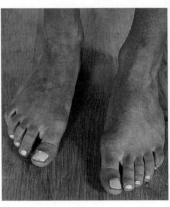

above The weight of the body should be equally spread between all four "corners" of the feet. Weakened muscles or rapid weight gain may have led the arches in the feet to collapse.

right Pilates works by strengthening the key postural muscles, making it physically more comfortable to maintain the correct alignment.

right Stand in front of the mirror and carefully check your posture. Pay special attention to your hips, arms, shoulders, spine and weight distribution.

when you begin to exercise; you will feel it most about 48 hours later. Stretching out the muscles at the end of a session helps, as can a hot bath. You may also want to try some of the wide variety of gels and creams designed to ease muscular tension. Ask your pharmacist for a recommendation.

So take up your stance in front of the mirror again. Only this time adopt what you consider to be "good posture". You should note the following points. Can you see them in your reflection?:

• Shoulders are level
• Hip bones are equal and symmetrical
• The thumb side of the hand faces forward
• The knee joints are symmetrical and face forwards
• The ankle joints are symmetrical
• The weight of the body is equally distributed between all four "corners" of the feet
• You are lengthening through your spine

below Become aware of how people respond more positively to you as your posture changes.

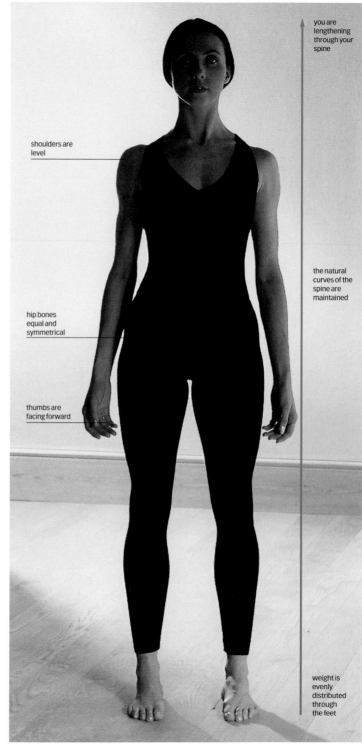

shoulders are level

you are lengthening through your spine

the natural curves of the spine are maintained

hip bones equal and symmetrical

thumbs are facing forward

weight is evenly distributed through the feet

making Pilates a part of your life

Pilates in Everyday Life

There would be little point in spending time exercising if you did not take a fresh look at your posture throughout the day, as you could still be reinforcing imbalances in the body that you are now dedicating time to amending. Pilates will help to strengthen and lengthen the muscles needed to maintain good posture but you also need to learn how to carry your body in the most efficient, safest way possible all the time.

Posture

Your posture, the way you hold yourself, says a lot about you. When you watch someone with very good posture enter a room, observe how your eye is drawn to them and the assumptions you can find yourself making about their lives. They seem to be in control, confident and capable.

Psychologically you are also affected by your own posture: notice how much more positive and alert you feel when you sit or stand upright. Try this when making a business telephone call, it will immediately give you more confidence. Everyone is naturally more drawn to someone who seems comfortable with themselves, and research shows that we consider people with good posture to be more attractive. But most of the time you are probably unaware of the way you carry your own body; most people think about their posture only when they start getting back aches and sore necks.

right Ask an honest friend to assess your posture as often we are unaware of our postural habits.

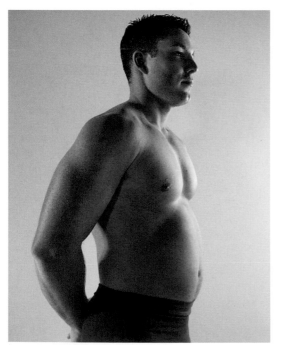

above Posture has a dramatic effect on our appearance. In this picture, the tone of the abdominal muscles has been completely abandoned. This lack of tone makes the model look slightly overweight.

above By correcting his posture and restoring tone in the abdominals, the model looks 5-6 lbs lighter. His whole appearance has changed, presenting a slimmer and more toned physique.

left Avoid flexing forward over your desk. Lengthen up through your spine with your shoulders back and down, and keep your head in alignment. Do not let the abdominals sag. Your feet should be flat on the floor, with your knees directly over them.

Posture is not just a question of how you walk or sit. To get maximum benefit from your exercise sessions, you need to get your whole body to work at maximum efficiency all the time so that it can cope with the daily demands placed on it. This means reducing imbalances throughout the body. There is little point in doing Pilates or any other form of exercise to improve your physique if you reinforce imbalances by using your body incorrectly the rest of the time.

Sitting

If, like a large percentage of the population, you work in an office, you are likely to sit for long periods of time, usually in chairs that are not ergonomically correct. Practically every chair in the western world has a back rest to accommodate our slouching. In Japan, where it is common practice to sit on the floor with no support, the incidence of back pain is far lower than the estimated 80% in the West.

If you are working at a computer, writing or eating, you are likely to sit in a forward flexed position, with shoulders forward, head dropping, neck muscles tensed and spine arched. Over a period of time, this posture can become the one that you adopt every time you sit, reinforcing the muscular imbalances. It is really quite difficult to sit up straight. Your torso must be strong enough to maintain a static contraction in the back and abdominal muscles to hold your body in place. Correct alignment is the same whether you are sitting, standing or lying down: it should not change because you change positions. Whether you are standing or sitting, the shoulders should be back and down, the chest open, the abdominals contracted, the chin parallel to the floor, the feet flat on the floor.

Pilates will give you the strength to maintain correct alignment for prolonged periods of sitting. When sitting, the knees should be bent at right angles and the spine straight and lengthened but still in neutral. The legs should not be crossed. This posture can be especially difficult to maintain if you are concentrating on an activity in front of you, such as using a computer. VDU monitors that tilt and stools designed to make you sit correctly are worthwhile investments. A good way to remember your posture throughout the day is to simply write the word "posture" on your screen saver: notice the instant effect seeing the word has on you. You can also try to enrol the help of work colleagues: ask them to remind you throughout the day of your posture and to correct you if you slip into negative habits.

Whatever you are doing, stand and stretch at least once every hour. Raise your arms above your head and very gently arch and curve your back. You will feel an immediate relief in the lower back.

Standing

Very few people stand with their weight distributed evenly between both feet. Usually they favour one leg and then the other if they are standing for long periods of time. People with an exaggerated curve in the lower back quite often lock their knees and allow their stomachs to protrude. These habits usually result in back and knee pain. Here again, it is important to strengthen the torso in order to be able to maintain correct alignment. Refer back to the posture check and try to become aware of the way you stand throughout the day. Make a list of your natural tendencies and aim to work on one thing at a time, until you gradually adjust your habits. If it helps, tell someone close to you that you are working on your posture and get them to remind you every time they see you slump or stand on one leg.

left Try to avoid curving the spine and bending at the hips when lifting a heavy object.

left Stand close to the object, then bend at the knees and take the weight through your legs. Keep your spine in neutral with your head in alignment and keep the abdominals strong.

above When standing up, try not to favour one leg but keep your weight evenly distributed through your feet. Lengthen up through your spine with your head in alignment and your spine in neutral. Keep your shoulders relaxed.

Climbing stairs

Everyone tends to lean forward from the hips when going upstairs or walking up an incline. A certain forward flexion is normal but this should not be exaggerated as it can result in lower back pain.

When you are walking up steps or climbing a hill it is important to maintain an abdominal contraction to help stabilize the torso. Although you need to see where you are stepping, try to keep your chin parallel with the floor. Glance down at the steps with your eyes; do not lower your head.

Lifting a heavy object

It is imperative to maintain stability in the torso when you are lifting anything, whether it is heavy or not. In some situations – such as catching a child who is about to fall – there is no time to prepare or brace the body for the force needed to lift an object suddenly. For this reason it is important to train the abdominal and back muscles so that they are used to contracting and the movement becomes an involuntary action.

When you do have time to prepare for the lifting of a heavy weight, bend your knees and lower the body with the torso almost erect. Place your body close to the object and use your legs, not your back, to give you the force to lift. Maintain the contraction in your abdominals the whole time, and try to lift the object from the lowest point possible. This will protect your back muscles from strain.

Exercises To Do During the Day

Apart from your regular Pilates sessions, there are some exercises you can do quickly and easily wherever you are. Reassess your posture throughout the day and practise the key posture points: you could even pin up a list of these and check through it from time to time. Maintaining the correct posture in your Pilates sessions helps to re-balance the body and achieve optimum results.

Drawing in the abdominals
Whenever you get the chance, practise contracting your abdominals by drawing navel to spine. This action not only tones the abdominals but will get you used to the centring movement often used in Pilates exercises.

right Keep your back straight and in neutral. Inhale and, imagining that you are wearing a tight pair of trousers, as you exhale pull your navel away from the waistband, making your waist smaller. Lengthen up through the spine.

Wrist circles
If you have been working on a computer it is helpful to give your wrists a stretch to make them feel looser. Remember to take a short break from your typing or writing every 20-30 minutes.

left Start by circling your hand. Support it with the other hand at your wrist if this feels comfortable. Circle in both directions, making a slow, full circle. Remember to keep the spine lengthened and the abdominals strong at all times.

Hand stretches
If you are working at a computer, writing or doing any other kind of repetitive movement with your hands during the day it can be beneficial to stop regularly and stretch out your hands.

left Keeping your hand straight and somewhat taut, draw your fingertips down towards the inside of your arm. Use the other hand to press them gently down. Now turn your hand in the other direction, drawing your fingernails towards your forearm.

Drawing the shoulder blades down the spine

This technique should be familiar from all your Pilates exercises. Standing or sitting, bring your arms to your sides with the thumbs facing forwards. Slide your shoulder blades down your spine, keeping them close to the back of the ribcage so that they are not sticking out. If you are not sure if they are sticking out or not, you can deliberately do the opposite and make your shoulder blades stick out.

right By gliding your shoulder blades down your spine, you will reduce the effect of any tension you are feeling in your neck and shoulders. Although hunching your shoulders up to your ears is a common reaction, it will exacerbate any discomfort you are already feeling in that area. Try to maintain the distance between your ear and shoulder at all times, unless otherwise stated. Throughout the day you can monitor the tension in your shoulders and try to become aware of situations that make them hunch up. For example, it is common for tension to increase when working at a computer for long periods of time, or when using the telephone, but by becoming aware of your habits and posture you can make a conscious and effective effort at reducing tension.

Neck stretch

When we sit for extended periods of time, especially while typing or writing, it is common to experience tension in the neck and shoulders. If you do store tension in your shoulders, it can be helpful to shrug your shoulders up to your ears, hold ... then let go. The following neck exercises will help to gently stretch and mobilize the muscles around the neck to help ease tension.

1 Keeping your spine in neutral and the abdominals strong, gently tip your head, letting your chin fall down towards your chest to feel a stretch in the back of your neck.

2 Turn your head slowly from side to side, taking care not to overstretch. Keep your abdominals strong and your spine in neutral.

Designing a Cardiovascular Programme

This section is intended to guide you through exercise in a healthy, balanced way. It deals mainly with Pilates-based exercises that will strengthen and stretch your body and give you better posture. However, in order to have a balanced programme and reach optimum fitness you also need to include exercise for the heart and lungs, known as cardiovascular exercise. There are three main components to a good fitness programme: strength work, flexibility training and cardiovascular exercise.

Cardiovascular exercise, also known as aerobic exercise, is necessary to stimulate the heart muscle. Regular cardio work will help reduce the incidence of certain diseases and will regulate blood pressure. It is also a great fat burner but this should not be your only objective.

You need to look at four important aspects of cardiovascular training when you are designing a programme: type of exercise, intensity, duration and frequency.

Type of exercise

To complement your Pilates training you can choose any kind of aerobic exercise that you enjoy doing and know that you will stick with. This could be walking, jogging, cycling, swimming, hiking, aerobic dance, step - the list is endless. The main point is that you should choose something that you will do consistently. It is no good saying that you are going to make rock-climbing your main form of exercise if you live in a city and do not have the time to travel.

If you prefer company, try to get friends to exercise with you, or join a club or gym that you like and that is convenient for you to travel to. You could book in just to use the sauna or get a beauty treatment if you want to check that a gym is right for you. Try classes on offer and ask for guidance from the staff. Team sports may appeal to you, or you could combine cardiovascular exercise with a practical skill such as martial arts. Home exercise equipment is

above Cardiovascular exercise can be practised cheaply and effectively in the home environment. Try power walking, exercise videos or jogging. You can even dig out your skipping rope.

widely available and need not be expensive: a skipping rope, for instance, costs very little.

Make a list of all the activities you feel you would enjoy and try them all. Cross training - doing a variety of exercise types - is advised, as the risk of injury from overuse is less and your motivation will be kept high. You will also notice that your list will get longer as you get stronger. You will feel more capable and confident about doing different forms of activity and you will enjoy them more.

Intensity

How hard you should work depends on your present fitness level. The fitter you are, the more intense your workout can be, but it is important to keep the intensity of the activity suitable for your fitness level and this is sometimes difficult if you are not used to working out. It might be hard for you to distinguish between muscle fatigue and systemic tiredness. If, for example, you are cycling and your legs ache from pedalling, you may think that the exercise is very intense when really it is the weakness of your legs that is making you tired, not your heart and lungs working hard. This becomes easier to recognize over time.

During exercise, music can really help to motivate you. Try not to choose music that brings back memories as this may distract you. Select something upbeat and positive that is not too slow.

Heart rate monitors are not essential but can be helpful in setting goals and record keeping. They are widely available and relatively inexpensive. They can also help to record recovery rates (the rate at which your heartbeat returns to normal after exercise) which document changes in fitness levels.

below Aim to do cardiovascular exercise three to five times a week. There is no minimum amount of time for exercise, so if you can only manage 10 minutes it is better than none and will help to keep you motivated.

ASSESSING EXERCISE INTENSITY

Here is a simple way of gauging the intensity of a workout. Think of a scale between 1 and 10, where 1 is no effort at all (resting) and 10 is the maximum effort that you can exert (an all-out sprint or a powerful jump). Everything else is somewhere in the middle. Remember that you are the one who subjectively puts a number to each intensity. Your number 4 might be your grandmother's number 8. Here is an example:

Mary is 38 years old, walks regularly and doesn't smoke. Her scale is:

Scale	Activity
1	Lying in bed (very, very easy)
3	Walking: 3kph/2mph (easy)
4	Walking: 5kph/3mph (getting less easy)
5	Slow jog: 7kph/4½mph (taxing)
6	Faster jog: 9.5kph/6mph (hard)
7	Running: 10.5kph/6½mph (harder)
8	Running fast: 12.5kph/7½mph (very hard)
10	All-out sprint: 15kph/9mph (very, very hard)

Simon is 55 years old, sedentary and a heavy smoker. His scale is:

Scale	Activity
1	Lying in bed (very, very easy)
3	Walking: 2kph/1¼mph (easy)
4	Walking: 3kph/2mph (getting less easy)
5	Walking: 4kph/2½mph (taxing)
6	Walking: 5kph/3mph (hard)
7	Slow jog: 7kph/4½mph (harder)
9	Faster jog: 8kph/5mph (very hard)
10	Slow run: 9 kph/5½mph (very, very hard)

What Mary perceives as being easy, Simon feels is somewhat hard, as the two are in different physical shapes.

When working aerobically, you should try to work between a four and an eight (somewhat hard to hard) on this scale. This means that the work should be a challenge, but not impossible. You should not feel as if you have been run over by a truck after your workout. If you do, you are probably working too hard. The fitter you get, the faster and harder you can work while still working between a four and an eight.

As you get fitter, you can play with this scale and sometimes may go past your last effort. This will help you to raise your threshold and prepare you for harder work with less effort. If you are out of condition, start gradually and work your way up. Do not make a heroic effort to win any races on your first day.

above Exercising in the fresh air makes you more alert and for those whose work is mostly indoors, being outside can help ease stress.

right Joining a gym or health club may keep you motivated, but don't worry if this does not appeal to you as there are plenty of home videos available with high-standard aerobic exercise programmes for you to try.

below Cross training (which simply means taking part in a variety of activities) is one of the most effective ways of keeping fit. It reduces the risk of injuries, keeps you motivated and gives you the opportunity to develop a variety of muscle groups.

Duration

The longer, harder and more often you exercise, the more benefits you will reap, up to a point. You will burn more fat, your lungs will become stronger, your heart will get more conditioned. However, you must start at a level at which you feel comfortable: it can be very demotivating to start off doing too much and getting injured, which could mean taking breaks in your fitness programme to recover.

The point where the disadvantages of exercise start overcoming the advantages will be different for every person. Some people have the genetics to withstand hard training, and they can make great athletes. Other people's bodies break down more easily and they should listen carefully to what their body is telling them.

Try to exercise for between 15 and 60 minutes. If you are in good shape, you can go up to the 60-minute mark. If you are just starting out, keep your workouts shorter (and less intense, of course). Remember that there is no minimum. If you can really only spare five minutes one day then this is still better than nothing.

Nothing is set in stone. Do not feel that you must exercise for unrealistically long amounts of time. Set duration goals that you will be comfortable with. It is better to

do 20 minutes every other day than two bouts of 45 minutes and then never again. Obviously, the duration will be directly related to the intensity of the exercise. If you work at high intensity, you will not be able to work for very long and vice versa. Beginners should aim for longer duration with less intensity until they are strong enough to work a little harder.

Frequency

How often should you do aerobic exercise? Again, you must remember that added frequency will result in greater benefits. Three to four times a week is desirable, always allowing one day of rest in between. This rest day can be active, however: you do not need to stop moving, just change what you are doing. For example, if you walk briskly on Monday you can do Pilates on Tuesday. You are resting from your cardiovascular work but it is an active rest. Consistency is a key factor in maintaining your fitness level.

To get better results, try to do aerobic exercise at least three times a week and make the rest of your life as active as possible. This could mean taking the stairs whenever you can, walking up escalators or parking the car further away from your destination, or getting off the bus a stop or two earlier. Your daytime activity does make a difference and can be classesd as exercise if it is challenging for you. Walking to or from work can be a wonderful way to relax and unwind.

If you are going to be running or power-walking, start with a warm-up then go at a gentle pace for 3-5 minutes before increasing the pace slightly, giving your body time to adjust. Here is an example of a running programme for a beginner:

above Cardiovascular exercise need not be boring. Dancing the night away burns up many calories.

Week 1: Jog for 1 minute walk for
    2 minutes
Week 2: Jog for 2 minutes walk for
    2 minutes
Week 3: Jog for 3 minutes walk for
    2 minutes
Week 4: Jog for 4 minutes walk for
    2 minutes
Week 5: Jog for 5 minutes walk for
    1 minute
Week 6: Jog for 6 minutes walk for
    1 minute

The total amount of time you spend on this pattern will depend on how fit you are. Twenty minutes would be great but if you can only cope with 10 minutes or less, this is fine - work at your own level. Once you start you will be surprised at how quickly you can progress to jogging for 60 minutes. Carry on adding a minute week by week, decreasing your walking time, until you have reached a satisfying standard. It is important to keep setting yourself goals. Make sure you drink plenty of water before and after your run and never skimp on your warm-up or stretches as this may increase your chance of injury.

left Exercising with a friend can help to keep you motivated. Make regular times to exercise and choose someone with similar objectives.

Preparing the Body for Cardiovascular Exercise

Warming up the body before exercise is vital to prepare it for the work that it will be asked to do. In the case of cardiovascular work you must warm up the respiratory system (heart and lungs) as well as your muscles, to help reduce the risk of injury and to focus psychologically. In a warm-up it is a good idea to simulate the exercises that will be performed during the main part of the workout, but at a much less intense level, to prepare the body gradually. As in the case of Pilates, the warm-up helps to set the mood. For cardiovascular work this needs to be faster paced: it can help to listen to upbeat music, probably slightly louder than for Pilates. When you have completed the warm-up and the stretches, start your session slowly: walk for a few minutes then build up your speed and jog. Ease your body into activity. If you begin too ambitiously you may increase your risk of injury.

The warm-up
This general warm-up could be used for jogging, power-walking (fast-paced walking), skipping or dancing. Always warm up to prepare the body for activity, both mentally and physically.

One leg circles
This mobilizing Pilates movement helps to loosen the hip joint. Work at whichever level you are accustomed to in your Pilates sessions. Repeat five times in each direction then change legs. Remember to lengthen up through your leg and keep your spine in neutral.

right Lying on your back, circle one leg, keeping your hips very still. Start with small circles then increase the size, controlling the movement with your abdominals.

Knee hinges
This will mobilize your knees and warm up your ankles. Keep your spine in neutral and your abdominals strong throughout the movement. Relax your shoulders and neck. Repeat five times on each leg.

1 Lie on your back in the relaxation position. Lift one leg so that your thigh is at right-angles to the floor. Point your toe as you raise your foot.

2 When the leg straightens flex your foot. Push your heel up towards the ceiling, then lower the foot. Think of your knee as a hinge, keeping the thigh still and limiting any movement in the hips. Exhale as you lift, inhale as you lower.

Ankle circles

This will give you a wonderful loose feeling in your ankles and really wake them up. Repeat five times in each direction then change legs.

right Lie in the same position as for Knee Hinges, but this time rest one leg on the other. Slowly circle your ankle in one direction, then the other. Keep your toes pointed and make a full circle. Concentrate on the shape you are forming and perform this movement as slowly as you can bear. Keep the spine in neutral.

Stretches

As a guide, you should hold each of these stretches for 30 seconds, but if you want to increase your flexibility or if you are particularly stiff in any area you can hold the stretch for longer. Make sure you stretch both legs equally.

Gluteals stretch

You should not only tone the buttocks but also stretch it for best effect. Stretching lengthens the muscles and may help prevent injury. Stretch before and after cardiovascular exercise for optimum effect. It is also worth timing your stretching session occasionally as it is easy to rush through it when you are tired.

▲1 Lying in the relaxation position, place one leg across the other, holding the supporting thigh with your hands.

▲2 Exhale as you lift the supporting leg. Keep the abdominals strong throughout. Relax your neck and shoulders and do not overgrip.

Quadriceps stretch

The fronts of the thighs tend to get quite tight as you use them for most lower body activities. If they get overtight they can cause problems with the knees. The main mistake people make with this exercise is to bend at the hip, thus losing the stretch. If you find it difficult to hold your foot, loop a towel around it, and use this as an extension.

left Stand facing a wall or other support. Bend one leg and raise your heel towards your bottom, keeping your knees in line. Keep your abdominals hollowed. Exhale as you lift the leg. Watch for tension around the neck and shoulders, and keep your head in alignment.

Calf stretch

The calf muscles can get tight, especially if you do much walking or climb a lot of stairs.

above Standing up with your hands on your hips, take a big step forwards. Keep your spine in neutral and lengthen up. Push the back heel into the floor to feel a stretch in the back calf. Keep the abdominals hollowed and the head in alignment. If you cannot feel the stretch take a bigger step forwards.

Assisted hip flexor stretch

This stretch uses a chair for support, but make sure it does not slip. It is particularly good for runners, but many other people have tight hip flexors. You may feel the need to hold this stretch for longer than 30 seconds.

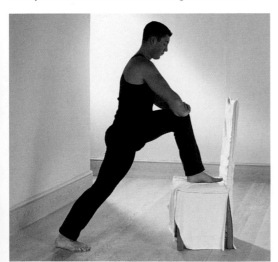

above Stand up and rest one foot on a chair (or something lower). Bend the leg and lean into the stretch on an exhalation, keeping your back heel on the floor. Keep your head in alignment, and your spine in neutral.

Adductor stretch

This is a good stretch for the inner thighs. Stretching all the muscles in the legs helps to prevent knee and spine problems.

above From standing, take a big step out to the side. Bend one leg so that the knee is over the heel and keep the other leg very straight. Don't collapse into the stretch: or let the abdominals sag. Exhale as you stretch and feel the inner thigh lengthen.

Assisted hamstring stretch

This is another stretch that benefits from an additional support. The hamstrings tend to be tight in most people, and can cause back pain if left inflexible. If they do feel tight hold the stretch for slightly longer.

above Standing on the floor, lift one leg and rest your foot on a support. Flex your foot and keep your leg straight, bending the supporting leg if this is more comfortable. Keep your head in alignment and your abdominals hollowed. Exhale as you ease into the stretch. Support just above the knee and try not to push down on your leg.

Nutrition: The Basics

Nutrition plays a huge part in how your body performs and how you feel about it. The more you know about food, the easier it becomes to follow a sound and sane diet.

Calories

People talk about how many calories there are in an apple or a piece of chocolate and they want to know how many calories they burn in exercise. But what is a calorie? One calorie is the amount of energy needed to raise the temperature of 1g water by 1°C. The same unit is used to measure the energy that food will give and the amount of energy used in activity.

Nutrients

Everything you eat or drink can be included under this common heading. Your diet should consist of a balance of proteins, carbohydrates and fats, together with small quantities of the other nutrients your body needs, such as vitamins and minerals.

Proteins are most commonly found in animal products such as meat, fish and milk, but are also found in vegetables, pulses and nuts. They help the body to repair and build tissue. According to most research, if you consume up to 15% of your total amount of calories per day as protein, you will have a balanced amount in your diet. Another way to calculate this is to allow 0.75g protein per day per kilogram of your body weight.

Each gram of protein is equivalent to four calories, so if you know how many grams of protein you are eating, multiply by four to find out the number of calories. Remember that 100g/4oz of meat is not equal to 100g/4oz of protein. Meat, like most foods, consists of a number of different nutrients, as well as water, which make up the total weight. Most packaged goods will have the nutrients listed in grams as well as the total number of calories.

above Not all types of fat are created equally. Some fats are essential so aim to eat monounsaturated fats, found in avocados, olive oil and fish.

The main difference between vegetable protein and animal protein is that the latter is what is called complete: that is, it contains all the essential animo acids, which are those elements the body needs to take in because it does not form them internally. Vegetable proteins (except for soya beans) are not complete unless they are intercombined (grains with beans for example), which means that vegetarians need to be careful to include the correct combinations in their diet. Try to choose low fat proteins such as chicken, fish and tofu. Limit red meat and other higher fat protein sources.

Carbohydrates are the nutrients that give you immediate energy. They are found in bread, pasta, rice and cereals as well as fruits and vegetables. You should aim to eat about 60% of your total calories in carbohydrates, but you need to differentiate between simple and complex carbohydrates. The first

right Wholegrain carbohydrates are preferable to refined starches as they are richer in vitamins and minerals. They help to increase energy and provide a little protein for muscle repair. This becomes even more important when you start an exercise programme.

right Try to include lots of fruit in your diet. Carrying fruit around with you will mean you always have access to a healthy snack and are less likely to rely on high-fat, fast foods. Being organised, not obsessive, is a key factor in healthy eating.

(such as sugar and honey) metabolize quickly in the body and their energy is quickly "used up". The slower-metaboliz-ing complex carbohydrates (such as pasta and rice) give you energy for longer periods of time, and at a much more even pace, maintaining a more constant blood sugar level than simple carbohydrates do.

Obviously, you should try to include more complex carbohydrates in your diet and fewer simple ones. The more refined (and usually sweet) a carbohydrate is, the simpler its composition. If possible, choose wholegrain cereals, brown rice and whole-meal pasta, which retain more of their original nutrients and also have the advantage of contributing fibre. Limit your intake of white flour, cakes and biscuits, as they tend to be high in sugar and fat. Also be aware that biscuits and cakes advertised as fat-free are not always healthier options as they can be loaded with artificial ingredients and sugar.

Fat is extremely concentrated in its energy power. One gram of fat equals nine calories; more than twice the amount of protein or carbohydrates. You need to take in fat for several reasons: it is an excellent, highly concentrated source of energy (a small amount of fat goes a long way, which was great for our ancestors but maybe not

such a prized quality today); vitamins A, D and E are stored in fat; it also makes food taste better and gives you a satisfied feeling. It is because fat tastes good that people end up eating too much of it and pumping many surplus calories into the body. Processed food manufacturers know this and add a lot of extra fat and sugar to their products to make them more appealing.

So how much fat should you consume? Most authorities agree that less than 30% of your total calories should come from fat. This may sound a lot, but almost all foods (including fruits and vegetables) contain some fat, so the calories keep piling up.

The average western diet contains around 40% fat. This, together with a lack of physical exercise, is the main reason for our spreading waistlines and the ever-increasing incidence of obesity-related illnesses. All foods will make you fat if you eat too much of them. However, fat will do the job fastest. The sum is simple: calories in (food) should equal calories out (activity). If one side of the equation does not balance the other, weight gain or weight loss occurs. All calo-ries that are not used will be stored. However, the storage process is easier for fat

left Include as many vegetables as you can with each meal. There are so many different types now available that it is easy to experiment for variety.

calories than for protein or carbohydrate calories. Fat likes to end up on your body, waiting to be used on that unlikely day when there is no food to be had.

Fat is not intrinsically bad, but all fat is not created equal. Saturated fats contribute to the production of low-density lipopro-teins, which cling on to the walls of your arteries, narrowing the passages and mak-ing them stiff and unpliable. The blood flows less freely and any particles that hap-pen to be floating through can get trapped, possibly causing a heart attack or stroke. The message is to stay away from saturated fats. These are recognizable as they are almost always solid at room temperature, such as butter, lard and other animal fat. Some vegetarian products are also high in fat. Trans fats, found in margarine and some cooking oils, should be limited, as high consumption can lead to obesity and other debilitating illnesses.

Polyunsaturated fats are thought to help prevent skin complaints, heart disease and cancer. Essential fatty acids are present in fish oils, evening primrose oil, walnut oil and other polyunsaturates. Monounsaturated fats, found in olive oil, avocados, fish and nuts, are considered superior to other fats as they are linked to a decreased risk of heart disease, cancer and obesity. Most of your fat con-sumption should be from this last group.

Eating For Life

Everyone has advice to give on eating, especially if it concerns losing weight, but very few can advise you on maintaining weight loss. Even if you find it easy to lose weight, it is very difficult to keep it off if you don't formulate a sound plan. Anyone can stick to a diet of grapefruit for a few days, or even a few weeks, but no one could or would want to maintain that kind of regime for the rest of their lives.

It can be psychologically traumatic for your weight to yo-yo. Not only must you cope with a sense of failure when you return to your average body weight, but those around you will perceive you as fighting a losing battle. It doesn't help you, but many take a great interest in other people's weight gains or losses.

When you lose weight rapidly through manipulating your diet – especially if your weight drops uncomfortably below your genetic size – and then inevitably return to your average body weight, the proportion of fat in your body may actually be higher than before. This is because some of the weight loss would normally have included lean muscle mass. Therefore you are making further problematic weight gain more likely, as lean muscle mass consumes more calories even when the body is at rest.

above Create time to sit and eat in a relaxed manner. Eating in a hurry can lead to eating poor foods.

left Try to involve your family and friends in your healthy eating habits. With their encouragement and support you are less likely to make poor choices. They may even have recipes or tips to share with you.

So what should you do if you want to lose some weight? First of all, you need to assess whether you really need to lose it. Not everyone is built like a supermodel: most bodies are designed with some extra padding, like a little warehouse ready for pregnancy or even for keeping warm in winter. No matter how hard you diet or exercise, you cannot fool your body's genetic programming. Those little fat storage areas are put there for a purpose; you may not be fond of them but they are part of your body.

This does not mean that you cannot improve your body. A sound diet and an exercise programme will make it strong. Your genes are a given but the way you treat your body will make a big difference.

Maintaining your weight

The amount of calories you need to eat depends on how active you are. You want to keep fuelling your body; keep it happy and give it what it works best on. If you reduce your calorie intake too far, your body will interpret this as starvation and will react by slowing down its metabolism to save energy.

The main thing to keep in mind is that this is not a slimming diet – it is a way of eating for the rest of your life. It must be pleasurable and you must be able to lead a normal life. The plan is actually very simple: just avoid those foods that you know are high in fat and "empty calories" for most of the time and allow yourself a little more leeway for the occasional indulgence.

above There are so many excellent healthy-eating books on the market that it is easy to choose delicious but nutritious recipes.

Reduce oils in your diet but do not avoid them completely. Extra virgin olive oil, for instance, is very beneficial, but fats, cheeses, and cream should be monitored. Alcohol (seven calories per gram) is another source of empty calories. This does not mean that you can never have another glass of wine: it just means that you should enjoy a glass of wine once a week instead of once a day.

Never say never again. That will only lead to frustration and anxiety. Chocolate is great, but it is very high in calories and should be enjoyed sparingly. Do not make it part of your daily diet but do not cut it out completely. If you do, you will end up dreaming about chocolate.

You should eat, and enjoy what you are eating. Food is one of the great pleasures of life. You should feel satisfied and not hungry or deprived. Think about filling up on foods that you can eat in larger quantities

UNDERSTANDING NUTRITIONAL INFORMATION

Try not to become obsessed with checking labels. Find products that taste good and satisfy your nutritional requirements, favour these then just check the labels of new foods. It can be psychologically damaging to over-analyse your diet – food should be enjoyed. Try to choose fresh, natural products, organically produced if possible. Beware of low fat processed foods as they can be full of additives, sugar and salt.

Fat

Food manufacturers may want you to believe that their products contain less fat than they really do. Take milk said to contain 2% fat. This actually means that fat makes up 2% of the total weight of the milk. But imagine a block of butter in a glass of water: if you measure fat as a fraction of weight, the butter (fat) is only a small percentage of the total. To measure the proportion of calories that come from fat, you need to know the total calories per serving and the weight of fat per serving. Take Brand X breakfast cereal:

Total calories per serving: 378

Grams of fat per serving: 14

There are 9 calories in a gram of fat, so 14 x 9 = 126. This is one-third of 378, so this product is 30% fat.

Calories

Calories are commonly listed in terms of serving size, which can be manipulated. The label on a chocolate bar may say it has 200 calories per portion, but there could be four portions in the bar. Some foods, such as avocados, are high in calories but also high in nutrients. Be sensible and base your choices on the percentage of fat, fibre and nutrients, rather than calories alone.

Sugar

Watch out for sugars that are not obvious, such as glucose, lactose or maltose. Of course, excessive sugar consumption not only causes dental problems but adds unwanted empty calories. A lot of fruit juices and carbonated drinks are full of sugar so try to stick to plain water for most of your daily liquid requirements.

Fibre

For a food to be classified as "high fibre" it should have a minimum of 5g of fibre per serving. Wholemeal foods, fruits, vegetables and pulses are all good sources. Fibre is important because it plays an important part in stabilizing weight and protecting against diseases such as bowel cancer.

without tipping the caloric equation. However, if you get the chocolate urge, go for it: anything else that you eat at that moment will not satisfy you. Just ask yourself if you really want to eat the whole bar or if a couple of squares would take away the

craving. Remember the 20% rule: if you only eat higher fat foods for 20% of the time you will feel less guilty. You will be surprised if you really start listening to your body. Most people in the west eat because of mental rather than physical hunger.

Make sure that you are adequately hydrated during the day: sometimes when you feel hungry you are actually thirsty. Aim to drink 2 litres/3½ pints of water a day (this can include herbal teas) as, among other things, this will give you the added bonus of healthy glowing skin. If you are going to indulge in a treat, try to eat something that has nutritional value such as nuts, rather than empty calories such as sweets.

left Occasionally it is fine to eat foods that are high in fat. The key is balance. If you constantly deny yourself you will find your cravings increase.

Frequently Asked Questions and Answers

Will Pilates help me lose weight?
Losing weight - or rather fat - is a question of disrupting the energy balance, between calories in and calories out. A regular exercise programme will raise the body's metabolism, and although the amount of calories burnt per session may be quite small, over a period of time the average number of calories burnt will be greater. Pilates combined with a cardiovascular programme and a sensible diet will give you the results you desire.

I would like to get rid of the fat on my thighs and hips but every time I lose weight it goes from my face and breasts instead. What can I do to lose it from the right places?
Unfortunately, there is no such thing as spot-reducing. You cannot decide where you would like to remove fat, that is a decision that genetics takes for you. Many people think that by doing hundreds of abdominal exercises they will lose the fat around their middles but this is not the case. Just think about people who chew gum: if spot-reducing worked, they would have hollow cheeks! Instead of working incessantly on your lower body, you should also build up the upper body to draw attention away from the bottom half. Think what happens when you use shoulder pads - you look instantly slimmer.

I would like to start exercising again but last time I went to the gym I just got bulky and looked wider. I really dislike the current trend to be very muscular, can Pilates help?
Yes it can. Pilates builds long, lean muscles by keeping repetitions and resistance low. As it pays special attention to alignment, every move is designed to elongate as it strengthens, which is ideal for anyone who builds bulk easily. Think dancer's body rather than power-lifter's.

When will I start to see results? I have tried other programmes but I just cannot seem to stick with them long enough to see any real benefits.
If you are diligent about exercising and combine Pilates about three times a week with a cardiovascular programme and a sound diet, you should start seeing visible results within four weeks. Muscles you thought you did not have will peep through and your arms and legs will start to look more toned and streamlined. Your back will be stronger and your tummy may look flatter. However, the change won't only be visible. You will notice positive changes within yourself. You will start looking forward to your workouts and feel stronger in everything you do. You will sleep better and will most probably be in a better mood. Your aerobic sessions will become easier and you will be able to exercise for longer periods at a time. Give it a month: it's worth it.

above Regular Pilates practice will improve your strength and flexibility.

I have quite a sway back (lordosis) and frequently experience back pain just above the kidneys. Will Pilates aggravate that situation?
Anyone with an injury or back problem should seek medical advice before starting this or any exercise programme. Pilates is an excellent technique for correcting certain postural deviations and strengthening weaknesses. However, it should not be used as a remedial method unless supervised by a trained and certified professional. Pilates will aggravate a situation such as the lordosis described above if the movements are improperly executed.

I am worried about incontinence (urine leakage) when I work out. Are there any exercises to prevent this?
The muscles of the pelvic floor can weaken, especially after giving birth. Like any other muscle, these can be strengthened to prevent the problem of incontinence. During urination, stop the flow a few times. The muscles you are using are the pelvic floor muscles and this action is exactly what you should do to strengthen them. You can do this anywhere: on a bus, at the supermarket, standing in a queue at the bank. Read the section on pelvic floor muscles for more information.

I play golf every weekend and find that I often suffer from a stiff back and neck after a game. Which exercises would be helpful in relieving or preventing this?
Pilates is an excellent training method for golfers as the customary action in this sport is quite often a hazardous one for the back. You should follow the whole programme, as all the movements will be beneficial. You may be pleasantly surprised as you discover that your game is improving with your improved strength and flexibility.

I have never exercised at all but would like to start with this programme. Could this be dangerous? I am a 54-year-old woman, slightly overweight and a non-smoker.

You should seek medical advice before starting this or any other exercise programme if you have any injuries or risk factors. These would include coronary heart disease, diabetes, high blood pressure, high cholesterol, obesity, a heavy smoking habit or a very sedentary lifestyle. Women over 50 and sedentary men over 40 should also check with their doctors.

I am extremely thin and would like to gain a little weight. What can I do? Won't Pilates just make me look even slimmer?

You probably do not get much sympathy from others as this is the opposite of most people's problem. Most bodies are genetically programmed to store fat, but yours is designed to stay very lean. Try to take in extra calories whenever you can, but do not rely on empty calories from junk food. Drink fruit juices instead of soft drinks and carry nuts and dried fruits or other high-calorie but nutritious snacks with you at all times. You should still exercise to build muscle, to give you a more toned, stronger look. Keep your cardiovascular exercise to a moderate intensity.

I cannot seem to motivate myself to exercise or change my diet. I'd like to lose some weight and get a more toned body but I lack the stimulus.

It is important to set goals that are realistic, measurable, and with a definite time frame. This will help you to look forward and stop you from seeing fitness as unattainable. You can set both long- and short-term goals. For example, "Within four weeks I want to be able to do the Hundred without having to stop halfway," is both attainable and realistic. Another motivational tool is to make a written agreement with someone who you know will support your exercise regime. Write out a contract stating that you commit yourself to exercising X times per week for X weeks. Have the other person sign as well as yourself.

left Although we are not suggesting that you walk around balancing a book on your head, we are saying that regular Pilates practice will improve both your alignment and your posture.

above Pilates, combined with healthy eating and cardiovascular exercise, lengthens and stretches muscles creating a long, lean, strong physique.

Beware of people who may unconsciously want to sabotage your progress. Strange as it may seem, there are people who may not want you to succeed: friends who feel guilty about not taking care of themselves, mothers who are worried that you will do too much, jealous partners who worry that you will become too attractive to other people – odd, but true.

I am a single parent with no time for hobbies. I know I have to exercise but I often feel I have no free time.

When you have many demands on your time, it helps to examine all the reasons why you might choose to do something. Exercise can actually change your perspective, making you feel calmer and more in control. As they grow stronger, most people notice positive changes in their self-esteem and self-image. Headaches, backaches and depression can mysteriously disappear. With all these positive changes, exercise can become a treasured and necessary part of the day. Six weeks seems to be the point at which perspectives change. If you can reach a point where you feel you "want to" rather than "have to" exercise, it will take away the "chore" factor.

Don't forget that energy creates energy, and this will help you in your day-to-day activities. Pin up a big list of all the things that exercise will do for you, and keep it positive. For example, rather than saying "I want to be a size 10" say "I want to be confident and comfortable in my body". Do not underestimate the power of words and positive thought. Use affirmations to make you feel powerful. Sometimes it also helps to remind yourself that little is better than none at all, so start slowly and see what develops.

Yoga-Pilates

Jonathan Monks | THE ULTIMATE FUSION FOR
HEALTH AND FITNESS

Introduction

Yoga and Pilates are both usually regarded as separate disciplines, and are practised as such. Normally, time is spent defining their individual theories and their origins to give them a distinct identity. This provides us with security in that we know what we practise; it's something definable and safe. The fact is, however, that each discipline you learn is as individual as the teacher you learn it from. It may be yoga of one of the many different varieties or Pilates from a highly qualified instructor, but it is still about feelings that are particular to each individual, and the responses that they will have to a given set of physical feelings.

This section is all about you, your body and how you relate to it. There is no in-depth history, proof of origins, or philosophy. In this section I offer you a method by which to find sensations in your body along with opportunities to feel and respond to them. It will allow you to create your own personal style – a personal form of exercise that you can take up, adapt and practise, wherever you are, whatever you are doing.

Why this section works

The information in this section can work only if you feel your body and begin to use it properly. This means that you have to practise regularly, taking an interest in what you are doing when you are doing it, not just going through the motions with the aim that all will be fine in the end. Pay attention to how you feel when you practise; are you a morning or evening person? Do you need twenty minutes practice every day or a thorough hour every other day? Only you can truly say what feels best for you.

I offer the contents of this section to young and old alike, but always with the aim of getting you to understand your body from the inside. When this happens I have seen long-term neck pain disappear in five minutes. I have seen better posture emerge through simple feeling and understanding in half an hour, and clients have dropped a clothes size in between three and six months. However, this is somewhat irrelevant for two reasons. The first is that these people have decided to practise because they enjoy it. They have changed their diet and drinking habits because they have felt they wanted to. They have grown into their bodies and now enjoy life through their bodies. The second reason why other people's stories are irrelevant is because they are not you. Be your own story: be your own body. Everything you've been looking for – the body beautiful – literally lies at your fingertips.

How to use this section

Read this section and, when you are ready, try it out and have a go. Try to exercise every day, even if it is only for a short period of time – little and often is best to start with. However, if you don't understand anything, take the time to reread that chapter, and break down the sentences until you

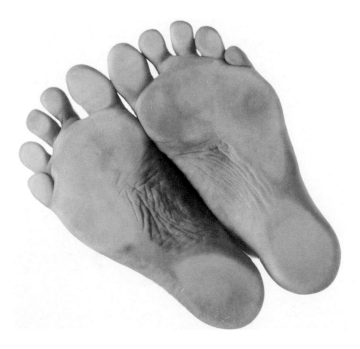

left It's hard to know where to begin on the journey of discovering your body, so I suggest you start off with what you truly know and feel. Take some time to discover how you use the ground beneath you, for in that knowledge you can unearth how and why you move.

can identify the body parts and movements I describe. You will find no visualizations or imaginative descriptions to aid you, since all this does is push your concentration farther inside your mind, the opposite direction of where all the action is actually going on: inside your body. Go through the first chapter, Core Strength, and become familiar with those sensations before you move on to the main postures.

Solid Grounding, is dedicated to reflecting on the imperfections of your body, and various ways of dealing with them. If you use this information in combination with the rest of the chapter on Core Strength, you may find the rare combination of stability and balance that solves your particular problems.

The chapter on sequences provides some ideal warm-up routines for you to begin with, but once again, be honest about the sensations your body is registering. If you find something hard work, try the easier option, and perhaps try it again the following day until it becomes easier. If you find it too easy, then spend more time in each posture, or try the harder option, extending your sequences for as long as you can manage to build stamina. Take a deep breath and begin your journey towards a stronger, leaner body.

A note on breathing

The subject of breathing fills many books. Such an important issue demands great attention. So how should you breathe? You have done a great job until now, because you are still here, but can you answer the questions, "How do I breathe?" and, "Where do I breathe from and to?" Pay attention to what you find.

Breathing is a marvellous way of removing toxins from the body. My own experience has taught me that sitting still and breathing deeply after an enjoyable (and indulgent) night out has helped me to feel a lot less cloudy headed. So pay attention to how you feel when you breathe a certain way. Use your breath to enhance your life.

Anatomically, remember that your ribs (which hold your lungs) are primarily behind you. See if you can breathe into your back and be aware of your response.

What you need

Yourself and an even floor are the essentials. A yoga mat is helpful, but by no means indispensable. Just make sure that the mat, rug or towel you have chosen stops your legs from slipping, to prevent unexpected split postures.

As for clothes, wear anything you find comfortable. I recommend a warm room and your underwear, since this is comfortable and allows you to watch your body move.

Listen to your body. It will tell you when you prefer to practise, but a good tip is that an empty stomach is less distracting than a full one.

Apart from these guidelines, you are your own boss. If spending lots of money helps to inspire you to practise then spend away, but remember – all you need is you and the floor.

A serious note on safety

This section is an outline of instructions. It is not a one-to-one personal training session. It cannot watch you or tell you when you are going too far, not working hard enough or using the wrong set of muscles. Only you can do this. Only you can check to see if the weight of your body is in your hips, not your lower back; if your knee is in line with your big toe and hip; if the pain you are feeling is that of muscle burn or a sharp pain that comes from a ligament strain or tear. Take responsibility for yourself; it is much more empowering in the long run. Take your time: feel. There are plenty of reminders along the way.

below These close-ups of parts of the body need to be joined together in order to see the bigger picture, then we are able to see how one thing can relate to another.

Core
Strength

Strength in the centre of the body enables all the other parts to operate more easily. Learn how it feels to pull in the muscles of the abdomen. Combine this with flexibility in the hips and strength in the back, and you are on your way back to the centre of your body.

Flexibility or Strength

core strength

below Flexibility and strength go inextricably together. As bent, twisted and constricted as some of these postures may appear, the purpose is to help your body find its natural line and balance. Strong joints are the most supple, and strong muscles are the most elastic.

Try not to think of flexibility and strength as two quite separate concepts, or as an "either/or" option. The body is extremely clever so pay attention to what it is telling you.

Watch a young child standing, sitting and moving about freely and you will quickly recognize how far most adults have travelled from paying attention to their own bodies' guidance. Often, we are not even aware that we are setting an insidious pattern until it has become completely ingrained and we are suffering the effects of poor posture, tension and stress.

Flexibility comes from strength and the reason for this is simple. A joint sits between opposing muscles like a see-saw with the tight muscle holding the see-saw down. To create flexibility in a joint you must use the strength of the opposing muscle to stretch its partner.

The first reason why you have these problems is because the body has adapted itself to move, sit and hold itself in the way you have chosen (not how it may have told you to). So now it is the perfect manifestation of who and how you are. This is most obviously illustrated by the way we compensate for a physical injury, but it is actually also happening in ordinary, everyday life. The second reason is that the body tends to open up only when it truly feels safe to do so.

Releasing the body

There are three common methods of making the body feel safe and of releasing the tightness that hides a weakness. First, you can just collapse and relax, letting everything go, only to find precisely the same tensions and tightness return once you stop relaxing and re-adopt your habitual patterns and methods of movement. Second, you can have the tensions massaged, or manipulated, into letting go, but, once again, your habitual methods and patterns of movement will encourage the original tension back into your body. You could, however, create balance between your muscles, and since balance is most definitely safe, the body – your body – is more likely to open up and let go, altering your habitual patterns and methods of moving for the better. Only when a weakness is strengthened to balance a tense strength will the tension in the body be resolved.

As you practise, be aware of the imbalances in your body; learn to recognize them in everyday life so your work on the mat carries on all day, every day, changing your body from slouch to sleek. Until you balance the "see-saw" in everyday movement the imbalance will remain.

Try to be patient. Be honest about your weakness, then take time to strengthen it until your body makes it clear to you that the weakness is ready to let go.

Gravity – use the floor

What is the one thing that helps you stay on this planet? It is the same thing that shrinks us during the day and without which we would float away. Gravity beats us down and also provides us with all that we need to find a magical lift. Remember Isaac Newton: for every action there is an equal and opposite reaction. To find this lift up, against gravity's pull, all you need is a body and a floor.

No matter what part of your body is touching the floor or chair, you can find the lift up simply by pushing down a little. After all, we are designed with a foot that has natural balance owing to its arch and a spine that has curves to give us more spring. Gymnasts, yogis, dancers and athletes alike all perform feats that seem to defy gravity because they have found this lift.

More importantly than the ability to perform great feats, this lift shows us that you do not have to suffer under the seeming oppression of the weight of gravity. After all, if you measure yourself in the morning and again that evening there will be evidence that you have shrunk a little in between. This difference between the freedom and length of our spine before and after our day is a major reason why we get tired. The stress of gravity seems against us.

Push down to lift up

But how can levitation be achieved when gravity is so essential to all our lives? Well push down a little. Try and find where gravity is affecting your body, where the weak points are.

Try slouching when you sit and then pushing your bottom down on the seat. Stay there pushing and slouching until you feel the need to let go and you will find that there is a natural lift that accompanies the letting go. You will now feel upright and in line with gravity, not fighting against it. Try the same technique but standing this time and if the feeling remains elusive stay with the pushing and slowly let go with as much awareness as you can muster.

Feel this lift and as it becomes familiar let your actions and movements become filled and dictated by it; never slouching or stooping, always feeling a light long spine being filled with

a lift. If you take away the stress and energy used in struggling every day against gravity, you can see how much easier living would be.

So we can forget about the long fight with gravity, and instead give in and work with this beneficial force, to use it to our advantage. Regardless of whether you use this natural lift to leap like a gazelle, stand on one hand or levitate, it will mean that as you age – the one thing you cannot avoid – you will not stoop, bow or give in to the pull of gravity. You will grow old gracefully.

below You don't have to know about Newtonian mechanics to understand how to use gravity to give you a lift up. See how the hand and the foot both have natural arches, which act like springs pushing up against gravity. Try simply pushing them down and waiting to feel a natural lift in reply.

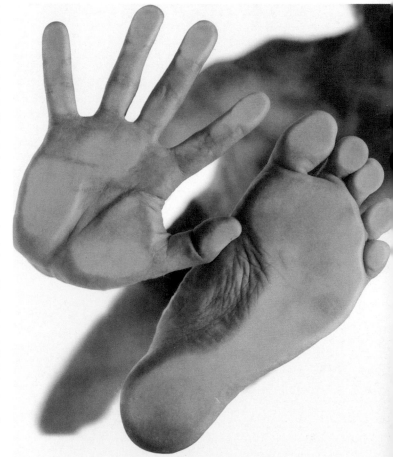

Pulling the Stomach In

The image of the body beautiful is constantly with us, whether in the media, with new looks of the rich and famous or in adverts for new and miraculous supplements or exercise fads. What is this image? Well it tends to have toned hips and legs with a pert bottom, a strong stomach and an open chest. Only the genetically gifted or determined fitness freaks seem to embody this ideal, and yet this is in fact how everyone is designed. We all have bigger muscles in our legs than our arms because nature intended us to use our legs as our means of transport. Around our middles are muscles in a similar shape to a girdle that hold our internal organs in the right place. Along our spines are muscles similar to struts that can hold the spine long. In the middle of our body we have a big hinge, the hips, surrounded and protected by big muscles (thighs, buttocks, hamstrings), which help us move around it.

So if we move using our hips as a hinge and our legs as support they will be fitter and toned. If we then hold ourselves upright using our "girdle" and maintain a long spine with our "struts" we will then not tend to let our stomachs bulge and our shoulders collapse.

Through rediscovering how our body is meant to move by feeling it from inside, the perfect body is achievable, and your own ideal body will emerge. You have to put time and intelligence into regular practice of course, but this can include walking, bending, playing games, entertaining and household chores, for they all involve you moving, and it is in this moving you can exercise, and enjoy discovering your body. Discovery does not have to be limited to set practice times for it is in the moments off the mat, sitting at your desk or doing the washing-up, that you understand the satisfaction of living correctly through your body.

Perhaps most interestingly, when you do start to move as you are meant to, your preconceptions of what you should look like fall away. An infinitely more satisfying feeling replaces them, that of a feeling of being at home within your own skin.

left To come out of the ape pose, really suck your stomach up and into your ribs. The position of the hips in relation to the spine is the reason we can walk tall. The more we can make our spine feel that it extends out of our hips, the more we will feel upright and evolved.

Ape or Man

Poor habits, sitting at a desk, leaning and slouching, can all result in standing incorrectly, putting strain on parts of the body. With poor posture, the weight of the world really does rest on your shoulders and will eventually push you into the ground.

1 Our bodies are remarkably similar to those of apes – we share similarly proportioned limbs and joints – and yet our posture is markedly different. Part of this is due to the way we use our spine, in particular our lower spine. Through playing at copying the stance of an ape we can understand how we became upright and perhaps more importantly what muscles are responsible for this step up in evolution.

To copy the ape stance, let your legs be slightly wider than hip-width as this will give your hips some space to move through, and let your arms hang down, opening your back. Give yourself permission to play and be silly; after all you will look ridiculous sticking your bottom out and letting your arms hang down, so you might as well have fun while you do it. To get back to an upright stance first try squeezing your buttocks and letting your hips come forwards. The feeling is almost as if the muscles of your bottom are pushing you forward (try not to slouch as you slowly stand upright). Repeat this as many times as you need to, until you begin to realize how important your bottom is.

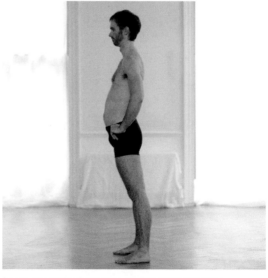

2 The variations on upright vary with perception and reality, especially when our habitual patterns constantly reaffirm themselves in our posture. Take this slouch as an example. The weight of the world is beginning to fall off the rounded shoulders, making life uncomfortable for both the shoulders and the world that sits on them.

3 Look, too, at the slump here, in which the weight of the world sits happily on the shoulders but all the pressure falls to the middle, which begins to bulge as a result. Practise coming in and out of ape until you begin to feel the hinging of your hips forwards and backwards, since this is the reason we can walk tall, without bulges.

Abdomen Tuck

Most of the stomach exercises we are used to performing seem to make the abdomen bulge out, but the core muscles of the body are made active by pulling in. Therefore, begin by lying flat on the floor on your front.

1 Rest your forehead on your hands and feel the weight of your body on the floor. Feel the front ribs and pelvis pressing into it. You are going to try to pull your stomach up off the floor, keeping your ribs and pelvis down.

2 Begin by simply pulling the tummy up and lowering it down. How high can you pull your stomach up from the floor? Can you feel the lower spine lengthen? Have you created a gap underneath your body? When you feel confident with this, move on.

▶ **4** Push your left hip and upper thigh up by squeezing the buttock and lifting your left foot off the floor. Is your tummy still in? Repeat, inhaling alternate legs up, exhaling them down. Can you begin to feel that the tummy can remain in, while the lower spine is kept long, even when you move your legs? Try to gain control of those pulling-in muscles as your limbs are moving.

Lengthen the raised leg from the thigh, as opposed to lifting by squeezing the buttocks. This exercise has the advantages of pulling your tummy in and of relieving tension from the front of your hips – a major cause of lower back pain. It can also lift the buttocks and add shape in quite a short time. With this, and all the exercises in this book, be sure to feel the exercise, not just in your head but throughout your body, so that the sensations make sense.

3 Keep the lower ribs firmly grounded on the floor and your hip bones and pubic bone flat on the floor. Now pull your tummy in as high as you can. Feel the lower spine lengthen and push your legs straight – so straight that you feel your toes spread.

Stomach Curl

The pubic lift starts in the stomach. It is very easy just to squeeze your bottom to tuck in your tailbone, which provides the same action. Pay attention to the feeling of the correct action – allowing pressure to be equally distributed throughout the body will relieve problems.

1 Sit with the soles of your feet on the floor and your knees in the air. Sit up as high as you can, pushing your sitting bones down into the floor. Cup your hands on your knees, so as not to use your arm strength to interfere with the exercise.

2 As you roll back, point your toes into the floor and feel your thighs work and lengthen and your knees push down towards the floor. As you come up, pull your heels towards your buttocks. The hamstrings and deep abdomen will engage to pull you up.

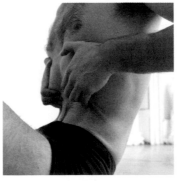

3 Look down at your stomach and pubic bone so you can see how you are moving. Using both hands, grab hold of your lower ribs and lift them up. Now suck in your stomach and all the muscles that connect from the pubic bone all the way up the front of the body.

4 As you roll backwards, keep lifting your ribs. You will find that your stomach will pull in as before, but now also up into your rib cage, making it possible to feel a lift in the body as you roll down. Try to detect the origin of the movement in the groin. The fact that the tummy pulls in so hard gives a feeling that the pubic bone is lifted, which in turn tucks the spine between the buttocks and rolls you down.

incorrect If you simply lean back, rather than roll back, the tummy will bulge. If the arms lengthen before the pubic bone has rolled up, you will know that you have simply leaned back from your chest. This will most probably be accompanied by your abdomen pushing out. The pressure here is in your lower back, not spread evenly in the body, and will cause you problems and pain eventually.

Elbow Lift

In this exercise extend through your legs to your feet, feeling the work in the thighs. Push your chest high off the floor so you can feel the space between your shoulder blades. This will strengthen your stomach muscles, and train them to hold your insides in.

1 Lie on your front and tuck your toes under your heels. Place your hands together, thumbs on your sternum, tucking your elbows in towards your ribs and then push yourself up to balance on your elbows and toes.

2 Lift your pubic bone into your stomach, as in the stomach curl. Practise pulling your abdomen in and up without sticking your bottom out, as that will disengage the stomach muscles, which is the part of you that this exercise is designed for.

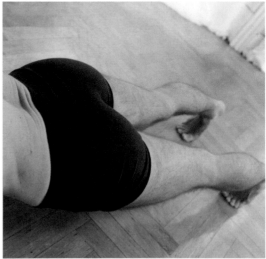

alternative If you find this too tricky, rest your knees on the floor, but make sure you really pull your pubic bone up into your stomach and lengthen the lower spine, or the hip flexors will get a good workout and nothing more.

incorrect This shows the classic collapse that usually happens when people try this exercise for the first time. The extremities, especially the toes, take the weight of the body and the lower spine collapses and will soon begin to feel the strain.

Hip Flexors

In medical circles, hip flexors are known as iliopsoas. They are very powerful muscles and especially easy to overuse. You will have noticed in the Abdomen Tuck how difficult it was to lift the leg while pushing the hip down. This is caused by tight hip flexors. When they become permanently tight, the hip bones are constantly being pulled down, emphasizing a lumbar curve in the spine. This leads to a tight lower back and disengages and weakens the abdominal muscles. For this reason, you may feel most tummy exercises in the legs, particularly in the tops of the thighs. However, the more you work on pulling your tummy in and lifting your pubic bone, the more you will feel the abdomen engage, not just during exercises for the stomach but in all your postures. This is the beginning of finding a lift inside you. Don't give in to gravity: be part of it.

Loosening the hips

The hips are probably the most important set of hinges in the human body. Protected and worked by the largest group of muscles in the body, they set us apart from all other animals by giving us the ability to move around and function completely upright. The great versatility of the hip joint means that we can lunge forwards (Forward Bend), backwards (Back Bend) and perform any number of combinations of movements involving our legs.

In order to provide independence of leg from torso, there must be a certain level of openness and flexibility within the hips. Constriction limits both the range of movement and the flow of energy. First, let's find out how to improve the flexibility of the hips.

A note for women

Wearing high heels tilts the pelvis forwards, bringing a strong contraction of the hip flexors and a pronounced arch to the lower spine. This not only weakens the lower abdomen and tightens the lower spine, but can also severely limit the range of motion within the hips.

left To feel like your body is truly fluid and free, learn to extend your limbs and make space between them and your body. Open the space at the back of your neck, between shoulders and ears, lift your tummy to help you extend your legs, and then all postures will begin to make more sense.

Diamond Curl

This exercise stretches the lower back and loosens the hips. However, if you are doing it properly and rolling from the public bone, you will feel the main stretch in the muscles of your legs, especially the hamstrings, which stretch down the back of the thigh.

1 Sit on the floor, as you did for the Stomach Curl, but with your legs in a diamond shape. Place your hands firmly on your knees, pushing them down towards the floor. Feel the hip girdle move firmly forwards and backwards as you roll from the pubic bone.

2 As you roll back, don't be afraid of using your hands. Grab hold of your knees firmly if you need to. Remember to roll your pelvis and feel the movement of your hips between your legs. No matter how flexible you are, there is always room for improvement.

3 Really lean forwards, using your hips as a hinge, and you will feel a tug in your hamstrings, the backs of your legs and the inner thighs, as you roll the hips up and over your legs.

incorrect Leading with your head rather than moving your hips forwards will not exercise your lower back or stretch your leg muscles. Shift your awareness away from your head, which is so accustomed to leading most of the time.

Assembly Position

Remember sitting cross-legged at school? This exercise is very good for increasing flexibility in the hip joints and the elasticity of the spine. It also helps to stretch and strengthen the buttocks. Try to repeat this sequence at least twice a day and you will notice the difference very quickly.

1 Sit cross-legged. Keep tall, pushing your sitting bones down into the floor to find a lift up inside your abdomen. Place your hands on your knees and lower the shoulders, keeping the neck, shoulders and jaw relaxed.

2 The important step now is to hinge forwards and over your legs from your hips, not by simply collapsing your spine. Lean forwards and pull your stomach in tight. You should feel as though you are pushing your sitting bones backwards into the floor.

3 Lie on your back and bring your knees up into your chest in the Baby position. Begin by rolling your knees, one hand on each, down into your chest. As you do this, keep your bottom, sacrum and tailbone on the floor. If you can do this, you will find that the stretch enters your lower spine and buttocks, just where it should be. Keep the work close to the joint, in the flesh, not the bone.

When you find that the lower spine has released a little, grab hold of your heels by taking your arms inside your legs, then slowly pull your knees down to the floor. You should again play the game of keeping your lower back and top buttocks on the floor.

advanced If that was easy for you, try this. Place the ankles on the opposite knees, crossing the shins, and lean forwards from the hips as before. If possible, place one shin directly upon the other. If this is very comfortable, then draw the knees together until the knees sit inside the shins. The more you lean the greater the stretch you will feel in the top of the thighs.

When you have finished lengthening over both legs and opening both hips, roll onto your back and assume the Baby position to complete the stretch.

Pubic Lift

The hip flexors dominate your range of movement in this exercise, by using the strength in your abdomen, and bringing you a greater tilt into or openness of the front of the hips. Don't confuse this lift with tucking in your sacrum, pay attention to lengthening your lower spine.

1 Begin in a kneeling position, knees placed directly under your hips. The feeling you are after here is one of lifting your pubic bone with your stomach muscles. Do not be afraid to grab, poke or hold on to bits of you to help feel and discover how your body works.

It is easy just to squeeze your buttocks and tuck your tail under. However, there is another way that will show you the relationship between your tummy and your lower spine. Pull your stomach in.

2 Pull your abdominal muscles in and up as hard as you can, so that your pubic bone is pulled up between your legs. Repeat this in blocks of up to 21 repetitions. You may inhale as you pull your stomach in and up, as this can activate the stomach deeper, so lifting the pubic bone higher. However, if you find it easier to use the out breath to lift and the in breath to lower, then do so.

incorrect Poking your chest out and leaning back slightly will leave your hips in the same position without moving your pelvis. Instead, try to pull your tummy in, especially above your pubic bone. If you cannot find this feeling then go back to pulling in and up. Keep practising and it will appear.

The Back – It's Behind You

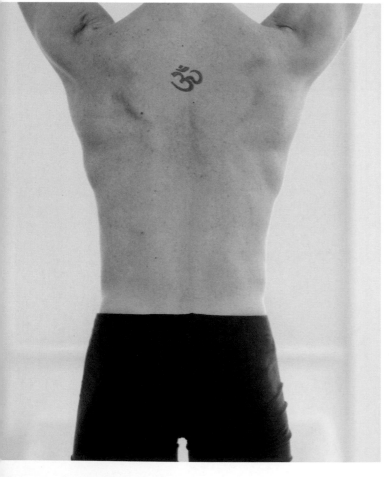

Your back is beautiful. It is the most amazing construction: 32 pillars stacked perfectly together, which not only hold your head high but also protect the spinal cord, allowing you to move your front so easily.

If we use our backs properly, we find we hinge in the right places. We hang our arms from our shoulders so that no tension is felt in the neck; we move with our backs so that our limbs are drawn into us, in a way that is centred, graceful and effortless. The back – our unseen part – can be our ultimate strength.

The problem is that our eyes point forwards and our backs are behind us. Consequently, we do not care for the one thing that we rely on – our backs. Since our backs are out of sight, they become out of mind to the extent that we cannot feel them; and if we cannot feel them, how can we be aware of changing or using them? The two main tools that you require to "find" your back are patience and practice.

Getting back to basics

Let's take a look at some games. First, can you lift your arms without using your neck muscles or the muscles that lie at the top of your chest or back? Most of us use the muscles at the top of the body, outside our core, to lift, pull, push or stabilize, whereas the body – which is very clever – has some muscles directly between the shoulder blades that can pull the shoulder blades down the back, so lifting the arms. What is the importance of this? Well, if you get neck ache, or even a headache, it is usually as a result of tension in the upper back and neck. Doesn't it make sense then that if there is no tension there, there will also be no pain? This simple exercise is one of the most fundamental steps in re-educating your body about where it stores its stress. The less stress that is stored around the head, the less stress is felt.

Raise your arms just above your head, so that your upper arms and body form a "Y" shape. Hold them there. Gradually your shoulders will open as the back gains strength, so less and less tension is felt in the top of the body. This will yield many benefits to your practice. Remember, the main reason behind all these exercises is to raise your awareness of your body, so try them out with the assurance that there is a purpose to them.

left Stand up straight and place your hands just above your head, with the arms active and outstretched. Keep your elbows bent and out to the sides. As you breathe regularly, feel your shoulders opening and the tension draining away from your upper body.

Ape Back

Lots of yoga postures were inspired by animals. This one mimics the ape. Copy the animal by leaning forwards and hanging your arms from your shoulder sockets as if your knuckles are about to drag on the floor. This will open your back and also relieve tension around the shoulders.

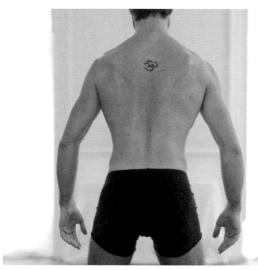

1 Let your body hang loose and you will feel all the weight in your legs from your hips to your bent knees. Your body should feel strong and open. But do not drop your chest, as this will pull all the weight of your head and upper body into your lower back muscles.

2 This profile captures the "dangle" aspect of the "ape man" pose. The chest is not drooping, so all the weight of the upper body is evenly distributed between all the back muscles that run along the spine and the legs and hips.

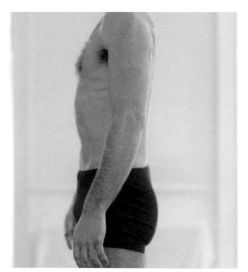

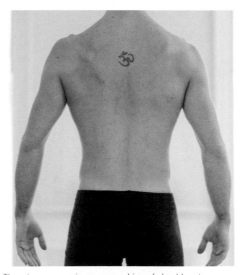

3 To get to the "man" part of this ape game is simple. Pull your tummy in and up hard so that this action will pull you into an upright posture. The challenge is to maintain that open feeling in between your shoulder blades and all the way down to your hands.

4 There is no squeezing or scrunching of shoulders to accompany the in and up tummy from "ape" to "man". In fact, the back hinges up in one long line from the hips without a bend, lean or slouch.

Drop the Chest and Feel the Lift

To lift the chest, you find the abdomen caves in and the back arches. However, there is another way. Let's return to training the abdomen. This exercise also helps to strengthen the muscles around the spine and relieves tension and aches in the back.

1 Lie on your front with your pubic bone and bottom ribs on the floor, lengthening the lower spine and engaging muscles of the stomach. Let your shoulder blades broaden and lift your elbows off the ground continuing to roll the shoulder blades down your back. Learn to recognize the feeling of an open chest and open back.

 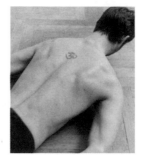

2 Now lengthen the back of your neck and continue to draw the shoulder blades down (you won't move much). The harder you contract the more the upper chest will lift. Keep your ribs and pubic bone down while lifting the stomach up. Simply inhale and try to lift the chest from the back and exhale, letting yourself down slowly.

3 Try to hold yourself up by the muscles that line the spine in between your shoulder blades and raise your legs alternately. Keep your tummy off the floor and raise the arms to the level of the body, but no more, palms uppermost.

Arm Lift

You can do this exercise standing up or sitting down, but, whichever you choose, it is worth checking yourself visually by watching the movement in a mirror. This will help you identify what you are feeling and allow you to take control of the way you move.

1 Begin with one arm and place the tip of the forefinger on your other hand on the end of your collar bone. Now simply lift your arm up until you find you are lifting your finger. Try to feel the shoulder blade drop down as you lift your arm.

When you have got the idea single armed, try with both arms, but watch and stop when either the top of the chest or the neck begins to become involved.

2 Relax your neck and shoulder muscles as you lift your arm. Looking in the mirror, notice the space that appears between your head and shoulder as you lift your arm. As you lower it, relax your neck and shoulder again and feel the tension disappear. Practise, raising the other arm in exactly the same way.

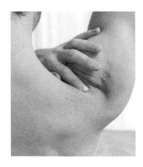

incorrect If your finger becomes squashed between the neck and shoulder, then you are not doing it correctly. In this picture the shoulder blades have lifted, and space is not being created in the armpit. Don't cheat, as this will stop you from feeling – the only way you will gain control and change the way you move.

Basic Back Bend

Now you have opened up the front of your hips, your lower spine should have lengthened down between the buttocks. All you need to do now is lengthen the rest of the spine on top of the hips and you will find yourself in a Back Bend without having bent your back.

1 Begin as you did in the Pubic Lift, kneeling down with your knees placed directly under your hips. Rest your hands on your hips.

2 Suck in your stomach muscles to lift the pubic bone up and through your thighs while you lift and extend your spine. This should keep your tummy tight and trim, and when you recognize that feeling, you can be sure that the spine is protected and long.

▶ **3** Place both hands on your upper chest and push your hands up with your body. Keep the back of your neck long. Do not stop the lift in your tummy and pubic bone. The chest should feel as though it is moving forwards and upwards, rather than downwards and backwards. If you feel pressure or discomfort in your lower spine or it feels as if your lower back is doing all the work, go back to opening up the front of your hips and thighs, as this is still limiting the extension of your lower back.

alternative If you find the Back Bend difficult, use your hands. Push your thumbs into your sacrum to help hinge the hips up and use your arms to help brace the back out long from the hips. If you feel pain or work in your lower spine, go back to practising Pubic Lifts.

incorrect If you do not lift your pubic bone and simply lean backwards you will find that the back will bend a lot but you will only move backwards a little.

Back to Front

How can you tell what's going on behind you? Can you feel when your back is long? Without the aid of some friendly angled mirrors it is almost impossible to see your back. However, you do have the advantage of having a perfectly good mirror that is always in view, called your stomach. When you stand or sit, watch how your front behaves; as these three examples show, it will help you see what is going on behind you.

1 Arching spine

First there is the time when your stomach sticks out, especially the portion below your navel. Try it out, let your stomach relax forwards and you will feel your lower back begin to arch (see the illustration below).

This is for the simple reason that your stomach is pulling it forwards, and if the spine remains in this pulled position for too long you will feel an ache in your lower spine. The obvious solution to this is to pull your tummy back in, which will in turn allow the spine to move back and your weight to be carried evenly between the front and the back.

2 High chest

Next, try pushing your ribs forwards. A squeezing together of the shoulder blades normally accompanies this projection of your rib cage, so try that as well if you wish. If you now pull your shoulder blades down you will feel a collapsing sensation in your spine. This is due the middle area now being compressed. Picture 2 showing the back view shows this pronounced dip, which is rather worrying when you consider that your kidneys are being compressed. To bring yourself back into line, place your hands on your ribs and pull your ribs away from your hands. Combine this action with allowing your chest to soften while keeping your upper back long to iron out that middle back dip.

3 Hip balance

You can often see on people with a pronounced hip imbalance that one side of the waist is longer than the other. When this is the case you can guarantee that one side of the spine is longer than the other, and probably twisting, which can lead to back and hip problems. To get your hip bones even, push the sitting bone on the raised side down whilst keeping that side of the waist long. Sitting on the floor, or on your heels, is probably one of the best positions to do this since the floor will bring awareness to your sitting bones.

Keep an eye on these three principals as you practise and you will be able to know how to see when your hips are balanced and your spine is long.

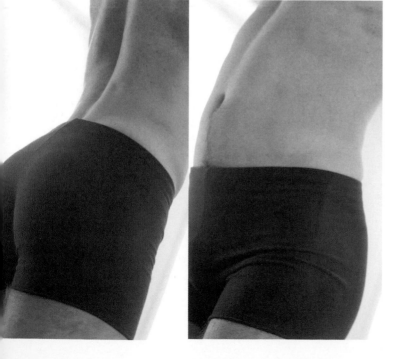

1 back and front If your tummy pushes out and your hips rock forwards, then you know that there is a lumbar curve in your back. This is how so many lower back problems begin. Lengthen the abdomen to lengthen the spine and relieve the pressure caused by this constriction.

Balancing the Spine

These three examples show common ways that the back is misaligned. You might only be alerted to this imbalance of the back by the state of your front. Once you become aware of the pitfalls, a protruding chest, or distended stomach will alert you to more serious problems.

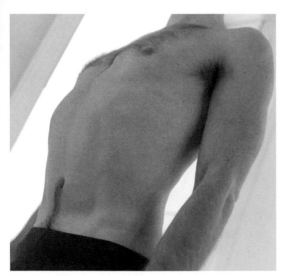

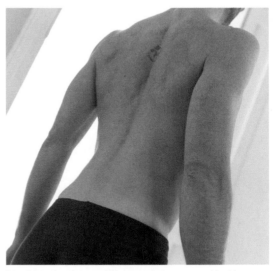

2 front If your chest puffs out and up, then you know you would see a heightened thoracic curve. You need to allow the chest to soften and the tummy to lift.

2 back Imagine that your kidneys are being squeezed by this curve in the lower back, and you will understand that it is worth correcting it. This is what happens when the chest is out.

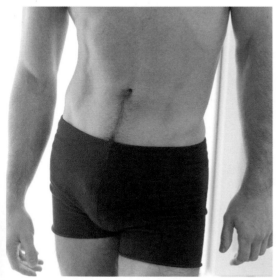

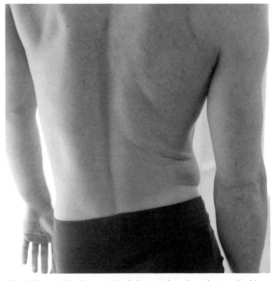

3 front If one side of your body protrudes and twists, it is merely mirroring the arc of your spine. You have to find out which of your sitting bones needs to lift, ground it, and then lift it into the rest of the body.

3 back If one side of your waist is longer than the other, as in this picture, then your spine is collapsing or bending to the opposing side. You need to push down the sitting bone to lengthen the waist to pull the spine back into line.

Solid Grounding

Even the most generally perfect bodies have at least one area that needs special attention. If you are reading this bemoaning how much of your body does not work, think about two things. First, your body is already fairly perfect because it has got you this far. Second, the work never stops for anyone; perfection is never achieved.

Be aware of the power of imbalances in the body. Continually repeating an action with an unbalanced shoulder or hip girdle will guarantee a habitual pattern that will twist and corrupt your body. You will not realize this until your body seems to give out for the smallest and most ridiculous of reasons: "I must have twisted strangely", or, "It happened just as I was getting out of bed."

However, the good news is that there are many bodies that have gone from being round-shouldered, humped, arched and twisted to long, open, lithe and strong. You will need to be constantly vigilant and aware, but with this will come the joy of truly knowing your own body, of truly knowing yourself.

It is recommended that you find an excellent physiotherapist, as he or she will aid your awareness of where you are habitually tight or soft. He or she will recommend exercises, probably quite similar to the ones in this book, which you must practise regularly. Simply having a diagnosis and a list of exercises is not enough; if you do not put these exercises into practice, you will not change.

Keep changing

Change the way you use your muscles, for they are the main reason why you are pulled out of shape. Your body is not set in stone. The only limit to change is you.

Do not be scared of treating your body to a session at the physiotherapist or masseur/se to loosen your muscles. If you invest in your body, it should run well for a lot longer: you do that for your car, after all. By taking your body to a specialist in bodies – whether a doctor, a physiotherapist, or a masseur/se – you can find out how to take an interest in your speciality. But whatever their advice, make sure that it makes sense in your body.

Take pride in being special. You have the best reason to become exceptional: to make your weakness your strength. If you can be brave enough to find, accept, know and love your weaknesses, you will find an inspiration that could unlock far more than the balancing of your hips.

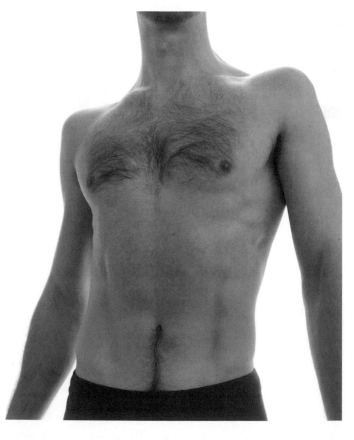

left Standing on one leg, wearing high-heeled shoes, slouching or sitting badly when you are working: all these things will contribute to poor posture. In the long run this may cause scoliosis, or curvature of the spine. It is never too late to take control of your habits, and your body.

Flat Feet – Flat Feeling

If your arches have collapsed then you will not be leaping around with a spring in your step. It is crucial to get your foundations correct, then you will have a stable support structure for the rest of your body.

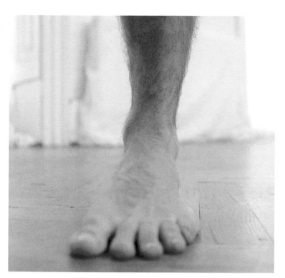

correct The ankle is in the middle of the foot with the toes spreading the weight of the body evenly across the entire ball and heel of the foot. When the foot looks like this, there is a natural spring to it, as opposed to flat and floor bound. To find this balance and placement of the ankle on the foot, have a look at the Jimmy Choo posture.

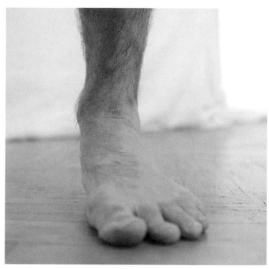

incorrect Look how the ankle bone is falling away from the centre of the foot. This collapse not only brings about a collapsed arch – flat feet – but also gradually pulls the big toe towards the outside of the foot. This will eventually affect the inside of the knee – knock knees – and then affect the hip as it travels up the leg.

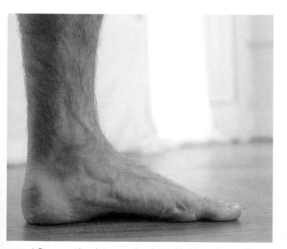

correct Compare the picture on the right with this and you will see the muscles in this foot holding up the arch and the ankle in the middle of the foot. The arch is there in most of us, but if it is not, in most cases it just requires us to condition the muscles of the foot for the arch to appear.

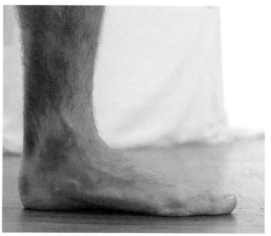

incorrect Look how little gap there is between the floor and the foot. In such little space, it is hard to feel a lift or bounce. The lift has to start where your body is in contact with the floor, and if the foot has collapsed, there will not be much lift. Try doing the Jimmy Choo exercises whenever you can to correct this condition.

Ankles, Knees and Hips

Let's begin with the ankles. Get a mirror and get honest. Have a good look. Which ankle corresponds to which picture?

You will probably find that one ankle lies differently from the other. When you stand, your feet probably do not point forwards at the same angle. This imbalance is repeated each time you step, walk or run, winding its way up through your knee to your hip and into your spine.

To correct the imbalance, let's use the mirror, your feet and some of your concentration.

Knees

Whether you are bow-legged or knock-kneed, by paying attention to the relationship between your ankles and your hips you can literally lengthen your legs. When you maintain the lift in your

arches, your ankles will not want to collapse. Down Dog is a perfect posture in which to work on knees and ankles. After all, you can look at them from the best position. Practise rolling your ankles and playing with the feet, until you feel the relationship between your hips and your heels.

Hips: learn to be here

When someone claims that one of their legs is longer than the other, it is almost always actually the case that they are holding one of their hips higher than the other. Do you cross one leg in preference to the other? Do you stand with your weight on one hip? These habits mirror and reinforce an existing imbalance. This is not to say that you must sit or stand properly on both sitting bones or feet for the rest of your days, only that you need to become aware of your body.

Go back to feeling. Are your hip bones even? Go back to the hip opening sequence at the beginning of the book.

The Jimmy Choo

This exercise is named after the designer of beautiful, but unfeasibly high-heeled shoes. it is designed to help you overcome fallen arches. Simply lift and lower your heels, keeping everything in line – it's harder than it sounds – and your feet should wake up. You can use something to help you balance, but if possible keep your hands on your hips and see if you can feel a lift in your tummy as you raise and lower yourself. This will bring your awareness to the connection between your feet and you.

left Down Dog is the best posture to examine the relationship between your feet, ankles and knees because you are looking straight at them. Play inside this posture. Try collapsing your ankles followed by bringing them into the middle of the foot. As you do, feel your knees move in and out of line and maybe even become aware of the use of the muscles in your groin. It is up to you to make time within this and all postures to learn how best your body works.

The Jimmy Choo

It really doesn't matter if you can't get your heels as high as is shown in the picture on the left. Push the balls of the big toes down and feel the lift of the heels up. As long as you feel this, you are heading in the right direction. With this feeling you will begin to make your foundations firm.

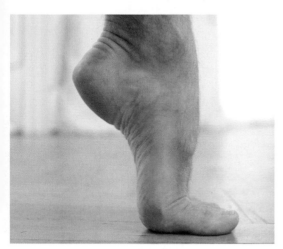

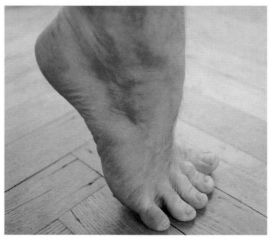

1 Stand with your feet facing forwards directly underneath your hips, everything perfectly parallel. Lift your heels up tall, on tiptoes (demi-point). Try to lift them directly above the balls of your big toes. Make sure that the ankles do not fall to the left or right and you will find that the feet are stimulated, the arch stretched and strengthened and strong lines formed from the foot through the ankle to the knee and hip.

2 Open your toes and spread them wide to give you a firm base, pressing them down to help you balance. When you have risen up and down on your toes enough to feel familiar with the action, concentrate on going straight up, trying not to lean forwards each time you lift up. Use the wall to help if you need to, but when you lift up directly, you will feel the direct stimulation of the arches of the feet.

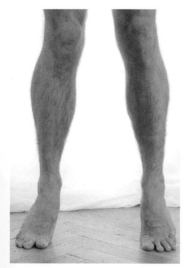

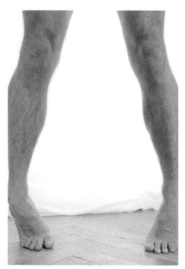

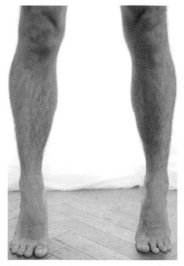

3 If your ankles collapse inwards stretch your little toes to keep your ankles in the middle of your body.

4 When your ankles fall out press the ball of your big toe into the floor and stretch your big toe forwards.

5 When both ankles are over the ball of your foot push your ankle forwards to help stimulate your arches.

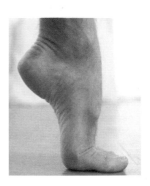

Standing
postures

Now you have found where the core strength of your body is centred, it is time to begin your practice with the standing postures. Some of these may be a challenge to your body, so begin gently and gradually build up, holding the poses for slightly longer periods of time.

Standing Start

By now you should have successfully figured out how to feel and use your core strength. You can hold yourself, warm up your body, move and, most important, feel when your body is working happily. Now it is time to challenge your body with standing postures.

To begin with, the demands made on the body by these postures will feel unnatural. But remember the idea of flow around the body. By using your core strength to hold you up, you begin to use the body as a pump to increase the flow of energy. So you should approach this section in two ways, looking at both individual shapes and postures and how you flow between them.

There are instructions on where you will feel each posture most, but it is important that you really look at the pictures and trust that your brain will make sense of them and interpret them into your body – it might help to use a mirror. Remember, there is no wrong feeling, only you, at that moment. If you look and read carefully you will have more than enough information to decide whether what you are doing is as beneficial as it can be. Bear in mind that you will fully feel a posture only after practice over time.

Flowing movement

The standing postures are designed to flow together. You can take a quick look through the book to see the bigger picture, but just as you are made up of little pieces, so is the sequence. Try to enjoy putting the sequence together, much as you might have enjoyed putting yourself together with your core in the first section.

Do not be scared to stop, play, or notice when something in you begins to feel. If you feel really comfortable, enjoy the feeling of your body working, flowing, not giving in to gravity. When a posture is hard, try the alternative version. When it is easy, stay longer, go deeper, extend further. If you feel discomfort, you should check that your core is working properly and that you are being true to your alignment and flexibility. Do not persist with a posture that is causing you pain, but carefully check the instructions and pictures again. Remember that almost all injuries happen when you are not listening, feeling and being honest.

left Build on your ability to feel and use your core strength as you move on to standing postures. After reading the instructions and looking at the photographs, listen to your own body as you practise the postures.

right Be aware of the flow of energy as you move from one standing posture to another and make use of your core strength to increase that flow. Not only will this be beneficial, it will also make your practice more enjoyable.

Lunge

Learn to love this posture. Inside it are myriad possibilities, all held static by the lift in the pubic bone and extensions through the thighs. The back heel in demi-point will stimulate the arch of the foot, which in turn allows you to open the hip. Lift the heel and drive the thigh back.

1 Stand with the feet together, extend forwards and touch the floor beside the feet with your fingertips. Look up, lifting the chest, and stretch one leg out behind you. Push one knee forwards and the other backwards (only one way makes sense) and feel the length between the back of your head and heel.

2 Place your hands on your knee as shown here. Put all your emphasis on lifting your pubic bone, lifting the back heel and opening the hip. The arms are down, but are your shoulder blades down too? This is the easy option, so if your legs are tired or if you want to give your tummy a helping hand, stop at this point.

▶ **3** Prop the shoulder blades to lift your arms and regain the feeling of freedom in the neck and shoulders. You should feel as though the torso is exactly the same as when standing, so the legs are required to hold you elegant and tall. The more power there is in your legs, the more lift and openness you will feel in the hips and body.

◀ **incorrect** The front thigh is lower, so all the weight of the body is being carried at the bottom of the lower back, instead of in the hip and thighs. The bulging tummy mirrors the overarched spine, something guaranteed to create an ache if held for too long. Notice also the back foot. Keep the hip and ankle happy by opening both.

Pert-buttocked Warrior

This posture carries straight on from the Lunge. Lower the arms to shoulder height from the full Lunge, and turn to face the side, rather than the front. This posture will help to open the hips, strengthen the legs and knees and reinforce the core strength that you have built up.

▶ **the full posture** From a Lunge, roll the back heel to the floor and allow the hip to follow. If you keep the front knee and hip in the same place you turn flat and into Pert Buttocked Warrior. The pertness comes from a lift in the pubic bone and a rolling backwards of the thigh muscles. This back view shows you the length of the spine which comes from the lift in the pubic bone, the evenness of the hips and the breadth of the back. Notice that the shoulder blades are down and that the neck is free.

◀ **close-up** Here is a close-up of the buttocks, because you need to really feel how lifting the pubic bone and rolling the thighs backwards affects the hips. Put your hands on your bottom and feel this work. You will also notice that the strength of this posture cannot fail to open even the most stubborn of closed hips. The right angle in the knee can be sacrificed for the sake of good buttocks, since stubborn hips are far more important to feel and open than trying for perfection without knowing where it is.

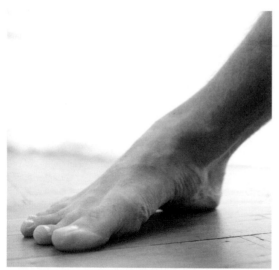

close-up The back foot is again very important. After it has been stimulated in the Lunge, you should keep a lift in the ankle while pushing the heel and ball of the big toe down. This will allow you to feel the body supported by both legs, rather than just by the front thigh. The more you can activate the muscles of the back leg, the easier it will be to feel the connection between the foot and groin. Try it and ground yourself. Through activating the arch of the back foot you will be able to feel the support of the back leg.

correct Look at the long line from the big toe to the knee to the hip. Notice also how the hips are facing flat to one side. Try to make yourself flat in this posture to benefit your hip flexibility and core strength and for the sake of your knee joint.

incorrect Look at the lines. See the stress on the inside of the front knee and how hard the outside of the shin has to work. The arch of the foot has also diminished. The back hip has rolled forwards so the hip cannot be opening as much.

Side Lunge

In this posture, the front leg has not changed position since the Lunge; the body has just moved around it. When the muscles work together, you will feel how they hold you long and upright and how the opposing forces of your legs provide balanced stability.

1 From the Warrior, lean the body towards the bent knee. Although the elbow is resting on the knee, the length is maintained along both sides of the waist. The hand on the bottom allows the sitting bone to be pulled backwards, and the knee to be pushed forwards.

2 In a simple Side Lunge the arm is lifted until the bicep reaches the nose. Notice the long line from head to heel, and the breadth to the back. Shoulder blades should be kept down and the back of the leg long. Beginners should stop at this stage of the posture.

close-up Notice how the length in the side of the waist is mirrored by that in the spine. The legs, both pushing forwards and pulling backwards, allow the hip to hinge and become stable at the same time, two opposing forces balancing one another to leave stillness. Remember your stomach: keep it off your thigh.

incorrect A nice try with the arms, but a lot of collapse everywhere else. See how the angle between the thigh and waist is not sharp, meaning that the spine has to bend to take the body over. The weight of the body is therefore being held by little muscles, those of the curved spine.

▶ **3** Raise the left arm above the head, keeping the shoulders relaxed and down. The angle from above demonstrates why this posture feels so good. Look at the line from the back of the head. It feels as though the line grows from the floor and allows the back to broaden and separate. Notice the gap between the arms and ears, meaning that tension is held away from the head.

Thigh Lunge

From the Side Lunge, turn the body to face the front foot. Body weight should be distributed equally between the front and back leg. It is called the Knee Trembler, because the weight of the body is directly over the front thigh and when this thigh gets tired the knee begins to tremble.

1 Keeping the back heel flat on the floor forces you to feel your inner thigh and back leg. Even though your hands and arms are helping to support your torso, keep your tummy up and in. Try not to collapse and stick your bottom out. Beginners can stop here.

2 Take your arms back like a bird, but spread your wings – your shoulder blades – to open your back. Remember that you are never trying to constrict the body, so squeezing your shoulder blades together to "fly" your arms back simply draws tension to your neck.

close-up This back view explains the essence of the posture. The length in the back must mean that the front of the body is long as well. Lean forward from the root of the back heel, but always keep your body free and let it hinge from the front knee and hips.

incorrect The collapse in the upper back means there is even more weight in the lower spine. If your back is feeling the weight, lift your chest and pull your tummy in until your thighs begin to burn gently. Notice how the shoulders are around the ears. Drop your shoulders and extend your neck. Remember the length from your head to your heel.

▶ **3** Raise the arms over the head. Notice that the neck is long, the shoulder blades are low, so again there is no tension in the neck. Notice how the tummy is drawn in and up, helping to maintain the length of the lower spine. Notice, too, the long, straight line through the body. Enjoy separating the knees – one forwards, the other back – and using your back to stabilize yourself. Here's a quick challenge. Can you use your tummy so that you feel buoyant?

Dog Split

This posture – a cross between Down Dog and the splits – is really quite tricky. My advice is just to go ahead and do the posture. Make sure that you stretch from your back heel to your top toes. In fact, once you're there, it is actually quite fun.

1 After the Thigh Lunge, place your hands on the floor and straighten your leg. Do not blindly push your knee straight, but push your heel down and lift your bottom up. Create some space and some lift off the floor. A quick challenge. Can you lift your leg up between your hands?

2 This is how the Dog Split is most often performed. The leg is lifted back until it makes a long line from wrist to toes. To lift the leg, squeeze your bottom and lengthen your hip. Try looking at your ankle over the bottom foot. Is there a line all the way from your big toe, ankle, knee and hip bone? Beginners, stop at this point.

incorrect This version of the posture is a common mistake. Inflexibility in the chest means that it is hard to keep the shoulders open and arms correctly positioned. A desire to lift the back leg high results in a lifted hip and an inability to detect whether the back leg is straight. The head is up, so welcoming neck tension, and the back heel is down, adding to the collapse.

▶ **3** Feel the floor under your hands and push all the way from your wrists to your toes. Keep your shoulders braced, even and away from your ears. Your hips should be even and your ribs slightly contracted.

◀ **advanced** You should not attempt this advanced version unless you can already do the splits. If you can, bounce the back foot forwards, root your heel and extend as much as you can through the front hip. Push your bottom up with your thigh (not with your arms, as this tends to lead to constriction), and your abdomen can help. You can use your head and a relaxed neck as a weight to pull the leg up.

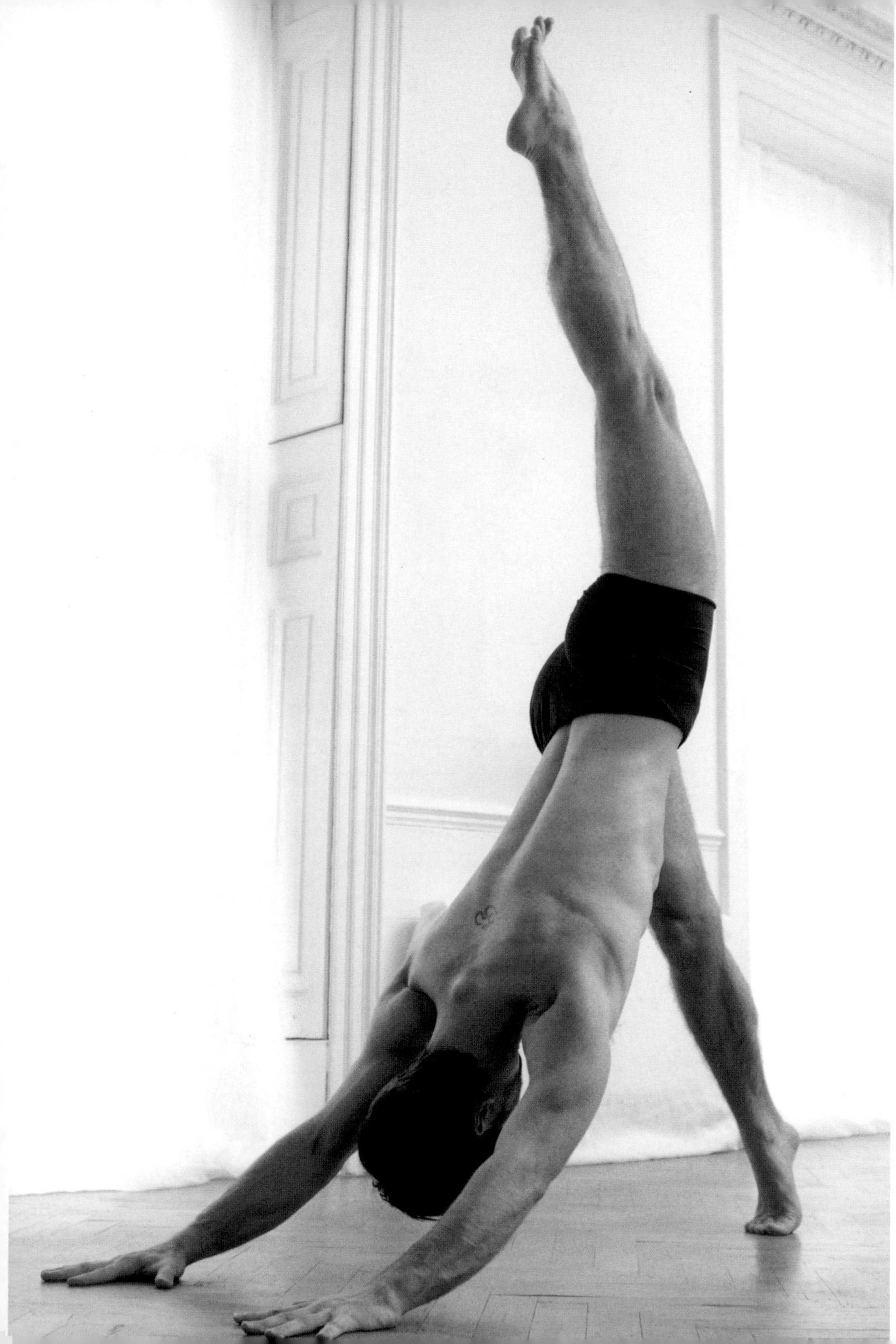

Press Up

This posture's very mechanical nature makes it a constant challenge. Sometimes known as the Staff pose, the body is held long by the torso muscles and, primarily in this posture, the back. If your shoulder blades pop up away from your ribs, try and perfect the easy version.

1 From the Dog Split, bring yourself to this position, pushing your chest high off the floor and lifting your pubic bone up into your abdomen. This will hold you up and away from the floor. To lower yourself, just bend your elbows, nothing else.

2 As you lower your body by bending the elbows, notice that the shoulder blades have not lifted and the chest is still lifted off the floor. Feel this posture in your tummy and back, not your shoulders and chest. If you are just beginning, keep your knees on the floor.

incorrect This is a case of being head bound – when you move your head you think that all of you has moved. People think that the most important part of this posture is to get down and so sacrifice all integrity to get there: collapsed shoulders, chest taking the weight, flaring elbows which detach the arms from any back strength, and a soggy middle.

▶ **3** The arms go no deeper than in this illustration, keeping the shoulders in line with the elbows. Any lower and the chest will constrict and the integrity of your shoulder stability will be compromised. This posture should have no constriction anywhere in the body; in fact, you should actively open your chest, shoulders and back.

close-up Your back is your strength in this posture. Tuck your shoulder blades down and away from each other to activate your back. Look at the shoulder and the muscle that leads to the neck; there is very little tension in there.

Up Dog

The more you understand the Press Up, the easier and more enjoyable Up Dog will become. Since the work was in the back in the Press Up, you now know just where to lift from to take you into this posture with your chest and shoulders open.

1 The width between the shoulders can be achieved only when the work is inside the back, allowing the chest to open. Notice how the tummy is pulled in and up. The elbows are open, rather than the arm, shoulder and back muscles taking the weight of the body.

2 The thighs are raised off the floor. The shoulders are wide, but follow the "V" shape down the abdomen and you can see that the muscles are pulled in and the pubic bone is lifted up, keeping the thighs off the ground.

▶ **3** See the breadth of the back. The shoulder blades are contained within the back and as wide as they can be to let the head float on top. The redness in the back shows the level of exertion. Use your shoulder blades to lift you and keep your tummy in and legs strong to protect your lower spine.

incorrect Can you spot the mistakes? The neck is not long, so something is wrong. The chest and shoulders are narrowed forwards, when this posture is meant to open them. The thighs are resting flat on the floor, offering no protection to the lower spine.

incorrect The head thrown back without any support means that the cervical (neck) vertebrae are compressed. It is obvious that the chest is not open, and the position of the arms means that there is little hope of involving the back to help lift. Get your wrists beneath your shoulders and push the floor away from you.

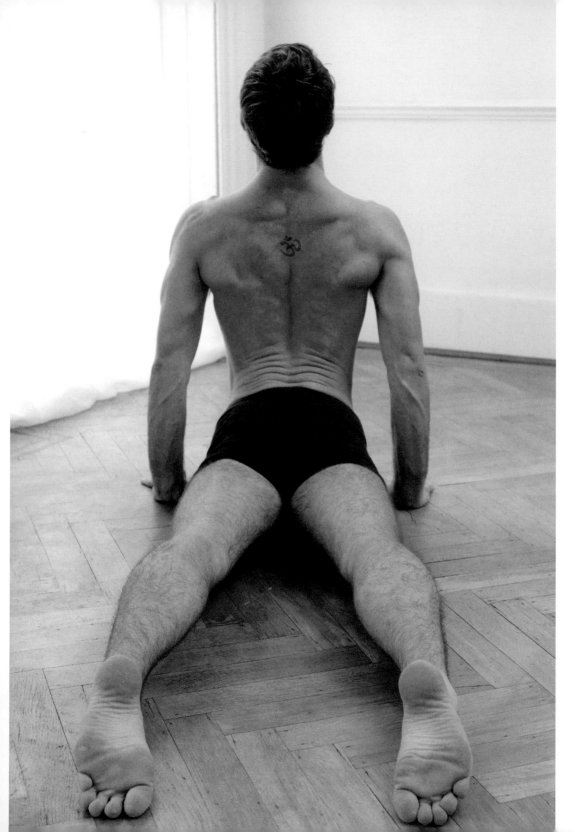

Down Dog

I would prefer to call this posture Bottom Up, for when the sitting bones come up, the lower spine extends and the abdomen lifts up to support the spine. Another name for this pose is Inverted V, and this picture shows the significance of the name.

◀ 1 Down Dog is not easy, as we have a tendency to narrow everything, especially when our legs complain at our bodies being at such a strange angle to them. To flow from Up Dog to here, just pull up the tummy, roll over the toes and push from the wrists to the bottom. Here, the heels do not yet reach the floor, since the Achilles tendons and calves are still rather tight. However, the shoulder blades are wide and away from the head. Keep an eye on your ankles. Is there a line from big toe to hip bones? Are the arches in your feet active?

▶ 2 See how little tension there is inside the back and shoulders. The neck can dangle free and the distance between the shoulders is as wide as possible. This means that any stretch in the chest is not felt at the expense of space and freedom inside the back. Broaden your back, open your shoulder blades and get your shoulders away from your ears. Don't be scared of taking your hands wider than your shoulders, as this will make these actions easier. Use the breadth in the back to open your chest.

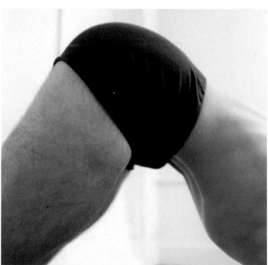

close-up Try really spiking your bottom up while pushing your heels down and keeping your stomach muscles lifted. Imagine the sitting bones up near the ceiling. This will keep you light on your hands, long in your spine and free in your hamstrings.

incorrect This demonstrates how not to do this posture. Look at the big curve in the back. This shows that this is more like an inverted "U" than a "V". The neck is long and dangling, but look at the tension in the shoulders. In this position you will find more weight in the wrists, whereas if you look at the close-up, left, you can see that most of the weight in the body should actually be felt in the hips. Don't worry about your heels. Lift your bottom and lengthen your spine.

incorrect This picture looks strong – look at all the activity around the upper back, neck and shoulders. But see how narrow the shoulder girdle is: the distance between the shoulders is minimal. How can this be considered an open posture? Look beyond the muscular appearance and see the constriction.

Jump

This Jump is the link between Down Dog and the Forward Bend. Any jump is a challenge until you know you can do it, so this is a lot easier to do when you believe your body will let you. Explode, fly, bounce your bottom in the air – gravity will help with the landing.

1 From Down Dog, bend your knees and push your bottom back and up. This should enable you to feel the leg muscles begin to work. Coil your body up as far away from your hands as possible. Pull in the tummy to hold the spine long and lift the heels high.

2 Push your legs straight up and see how high you can bounce. Lift your heels so your stomach pulls right in. Look at your tummy to see where it's gone. As silly as this may seem, it will help you pull higher off the floor, which in turn introduces you to feeling the lift.

3 Extend right through your hands and arms, since these are the struts that hold up the body when you spring forwards. You are less likely to collapse if you keep your arms strong. From the coiled back position, push your legs straight up, bouncing as high as you can.

incorrect This position says, "I'm scared". Notice the way the back is rounded, the shoulders are rolled in and the body is already heading towards the hands. How can you expect to bounce high from here if the spine is not long, the arms not strong and the thighs not curled to pounce? Try bouncing on the spot before bouncing forwards.

▶ **4** Here is how the feet should meet the floor – as though you have been folded in the middle. Stretch your legs all the way to your toes, so you feel you open up as you jump up. Suck your tummy in so hard that you feel you can stay up there. Aim to land with your feet in between the hands, ready for the Forward Bend on the following page. This position requires strength, balance and flexibility, and when you find them, your body can move and jump just as you imagine it can.

Forward Bend

On landing from your Jump, you are almost there. Find the hinge in the hips, and then allow both the backs of the legs and the lower back to lengthen from the top point. All you need to do is push your heels down and lift your bottom. It's that simple.

1 A Forward Bend does not require straight legs. Always keep your chest against your thighs to maintain the maximum length in your lower spine. Pull your tummy off your thighs to help you lengthen the lower spine. Then simply push your heels down and push your bottom up. Do not push your knees straight, unless they go easily, as all this will do is take the work away from your upper thighs.

2 Aim for a perfect hinge from your hips no matter how straight you can press your legs. All that pushing your legs backwards will achieve is taking your knee joint beyond the position where it functions most efficiently. Learn to carry the weight of your body in your hips, not in the backs of your knees. Allow your head to relax while you keep lifting your bottom.

incorrect This picture is just to remind you to keep your shoulders away from your head. Allow the back to broaden. It is so easy in your eagerness to bend down low to use the wrong muscles and take the effort and attention away from where it should be – in your hips. Use your legs to go forwards; they are a lot bigger and closer to the hip hinge than your arms.

▶ **3** If you find the Forward Bend easy, take your upper body out of the equation and lift your arms. Can you keep your back broad, your legs long and your chest on your thighs without the aid of your arms? Pull your stomach off your thighs, yet push your head and chest on to your legs. Feel the work in the thighs and abdomen, as this will strengthen the hips and, in turn, deepen the stretch.

incorrect This looks quite flexible and the hands are touching the floor, but look how the spine is bowing to achieve this. Here the hip hinge is wide open. This means the stress is carried in the back and knees, both a little more fragile than the hips and thighs. A Forward Bend does not require straight legs, it requires a movement of the hips towards the thighs.

Twisted
postures

These are positions to challenge the inside of your body as well as the outside. If you practise them regularly you will feel the benefits in your digestive system and also in your waistline, proving that true beauty starts from within.

Seated Twist and Prayer

It may take some time to become familiar with the sensation of space in your back, but keep searching for it because when you can apply it to a twist, you'll feel a freedom in your spine that you will want to keep.

◀ 1 Begin by standing upright and place your palms together at shoulder height, but as you do, keep as much distance between your elbows as possible. Keep this space as you bend your knees, sit down and twist, for it will help you to maintain some space between your thighs and tummy and also inside your back.

▶ 2 Think of taking your chest forwards and slightly up and your bottom backwards. Check that there is space between your hands and chest. Breathe into your back, breathe out and twist with your tummy. Keep the back of your neck long and remember that your neck is part of your spine, so that if it droops or twists away from that central line of the twist, you are more likely to injure it. Note how the heels, shins and toes are all kept together as a guide to help keep the hips in line. There should be no constrictions. The back is not designed entirely for the purpose of twisting, and twisting it when it is compressed is just silly.

close-up This angle shows the line of the spine. Take a look at where the twist comes from. The lower spine is long and flat, held safe by the tummy. Follow the line up and just underneath the tattoo where the smaller vertebrae of the thorax begin, the twist begins. Let your chest roll round. Use your breastbone as a guide if you cannot feel the twist. Can you keep the top shoulder blade open and the neck long?

incorrect Here we see a twist and droop. The spine is not extended, there is no twist to be seen and the middle of the back will feel the weight of this position. If you find yourself doing this, drop your bottom down and extend your chest. Remember, you have a long spine, so use its full length, otherwise you will begin to feel the strain.

advanced If you are able to do this Pelican pose, it is a good link into the next posture. Gaze at your foot (the one under your elbow) and curl the heel of your other foot towards your bottom. Keep your knees together, as this will help to maintain some stability in the hips and point that foot before getting ready to drive it back.

Revolved Lunge

Keep this posture simple and do not try to twist too far as you may end up losing all stability. Instead, concentrate on keeping your hips balanced and your back open and when this feels natural, begin to twist around by trying to move your belly button to face your thigh.

twisted postures

1 Having lifted the leg in the Pelican, drive it back as long as is comfortable while keeping that angle in the front knee. Holding your bottom will help you feel this strange sensation of pushing the knee forwards while pulling the hip backwards.

2 This angle shows you the space between the shoulder blades, which are free of constriction. It also shows the wrist under the shoulder and the bicep rolled forwards, since this helps to open the back and roll the shoulders down away from the ears.

close-up This close-up draws attention to the centre of this posture, because in the hurry to extend one leg back and one forwards, lift an arm and feel the floor with the opposite hand, it is easy to forget that you are revolving and that to do so you need your tummy to hold your centre still. Notice that the chest is open and yet the top arm follows the curl of the shoulder forward and is not just pushing up to the ceiling. Think from the centre out. Don't get distracted by your extremities.

incorrect There is a lovely line down the back but look at that top arm. Note how the back has constricted with the desire to find the ceiling. Follow the line of the top arm into the body and you will see that it passes straight out of the shoulder into thin air. It is not securely in the shoulder joint.

▶ **3** As you begin to twist around, be aware of the space beneath you and don't be tempted to droop and crush it. Just remember that when you pull the opposite ends of a twisted towel, it deepens the twist, so keep your chest up and forwards and your back leg driving backwards to create the effect in your body. Follow the line of the top arm and you will see it is carried directly through the shoulder joint. There is no constriction within the top shoulder blade and both the back and the chest are open. The back leg is extended as long as possible and yet all parts of the body are revolved around the middle. Pay attention to your core strength.

Side Triangle

When you balance on your side, you naturally think that your arm is supporting you. However, the arm does not need to do much work since its bones provide a solid staff. The side of your body is not so solid, so put your attention to using all the muscles down that side to make it stiff.

1 From the Revolved Lunge, put (or keep) your hand on your bottom, push down hard and lean back a little. Your leg will whip itself back in its desire to straighten. Pushing your legs, and keeping them long, and the stomach strong, will help to hold you up.

2 As a prelude to the advanced posture, try this version. Look at the twist in the middle. It requires all your core muscles – tummy, back and hips – to pull together so that you can push and lift at the same time.

alternative Any pain in the wrist, elbow or shoulder will warrant this amendment. However, just because you are using two hands to balance does not mean you can collapse through your middle. In fact, it means you should work your middle even harder.

incorrect You can lower yourself from the first posture to this and back up again, which is a nice exercise, but to hold this position will do little except help you to strain something. There is no space between head and neck and no sign of a lift against gravity. When people first try this version it is such hard work for them. Then, when they find their middle, they feel so much lighter.

▶ **advanced** This looks tough, but is really quite easy. In Side Triangle, make a big tunnel underneath you by pushing off the floor and sucking the side of your tummy up off the floor. Bend the knee so you can lift your top leg to grab hold of the big toe of the top foot. Then simply push the top leg straight while holding on to it. It may take a little time, but it's not that hard.

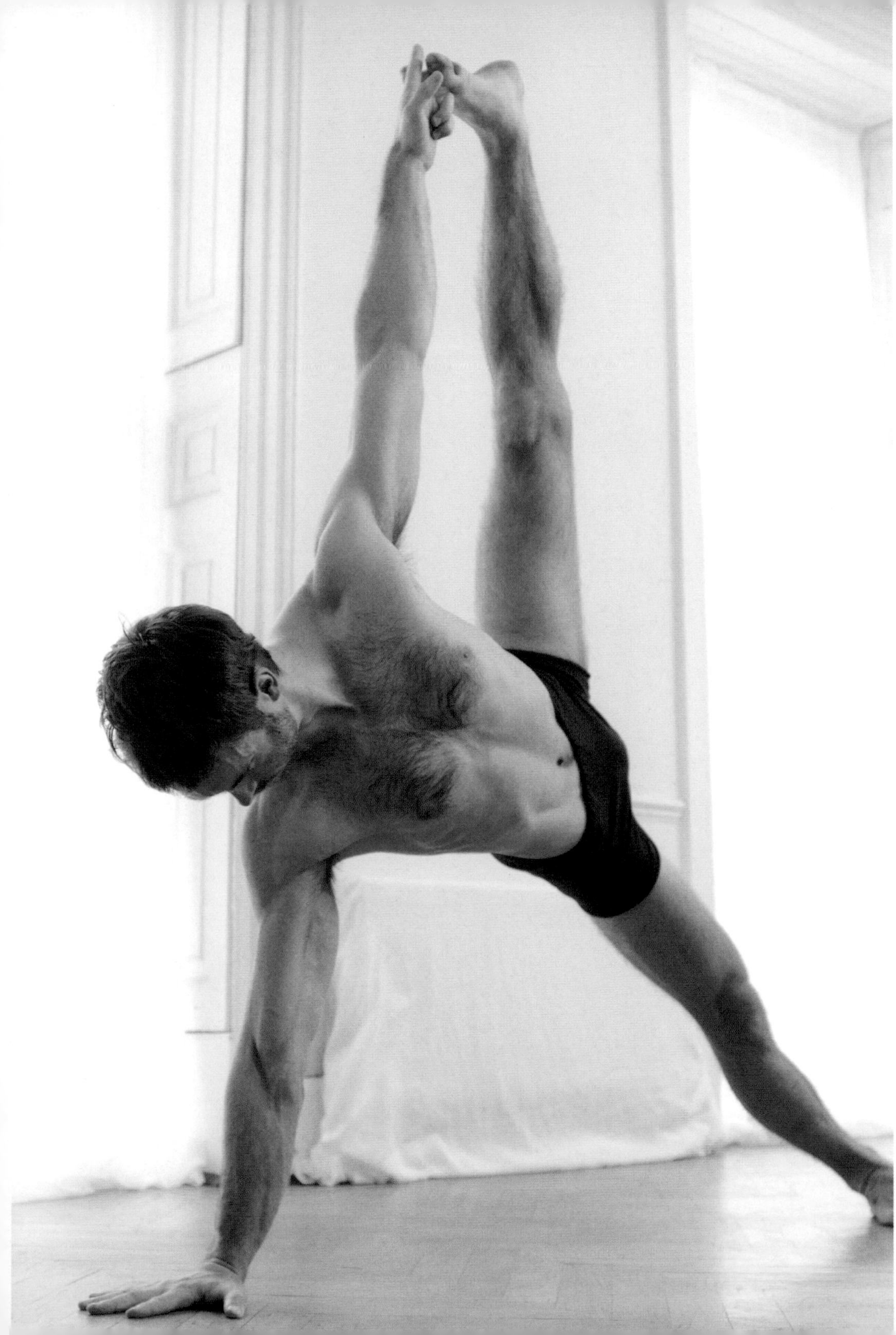

Triangle

With both feet back on the floor, turn to face the side, and you are in Triangle. This is also a twist which starts in the abdomen and ends in the neck, so practise rolling your body behind you, twisting away from the floor and looking up to the ceiling.

1 Holding the buttock of the front leg with the opposite hand, lift it to begin your descent into Triangle pose. Pay plenty of attention to the length in both sides of your waist. Use the same activation of your side tummy muscles as in the last posture.

2 Keep lifting your bottom up, hinging through your hip, until your hand reaches your shin, ankle or foot. Extend both sides of your body. Pull your tummy in and roll your chest back over your thighs. If you are really tight in the legs, place the hand higher.

incorrect Spot the mistakes. The hand is on the wrong buttock, meaning there is no biofeedback in the hamstring of the other leg, no matter how high she lifts. A curvy spine and tilt forwards means the effect of this posture is handed to the middle and lower back, instead of to the muscles of the hip. Lengthen, don't droop.

the correct alignment This shows you how your body ideally sits in line and over your leg. You may have no one to assist you but you still have the ability to close your front ribs and roll your chest backwards over your leg. This will keep your spine long.

▶ 3 How many triangles can you see? There are only two, but the importance of them explains the posture. The underside of the body is a straight line and both sides of the waist are even, which means the spine is kept long. Thus the flexibility for this posture comes from the muscles in the hips rather than from a bend in the back, as curves do not appear in a triangle. The other triangle – of the legs – shows how great this posture is for opening the hips. The hand is on the opposite sitting bone to help pull the bottom up and keep the hamstring of that front leg as long as possible. Don't be boxed in by this posture. Be a triangle.

Revolved Triangle

This is a difficult posture and should be approached intelligently. It demands great awareness and stability from your hips, while your core strength maintains a length to your lumbar spine and provides a twist above it. Take it slowly until all the parts work together.

◀ **1** From the Triangle, reverse the hands so the buttock is still being lifted, this time by the arm of the same side. The other arm goes to the shin, the ankle or maybe even the floor. Pull in your tummy well and be prepared to really feel the back of your front leg. Push your heel down and lift your bottom up to extend the front leg long. Keep your front long, as this will mean that the spine is more likely to remain long.

▶ **2** Now try placing the hand further down the leg, aiming for the floor by the little toe of the front foot. Look at the triangles in the posture and at the spine. The strength in the legs means that the hips are more likely to open to allow you deeper over your front leg. Really hold and lift your buttock, as this will help you to lengthen your lower spine and extend your chest forwards. Try to keep your back broad as you roll your chest backwards. Try pushing your sitting bone back into your hand while taking your chest forwards. What happens to your leg?

close-up The revolution of the twist is in the tummy. You can see the proof before you. Keep both sides of your waist long and twist. Then maintain this length by pushing your hand backwards. Give your sitting bone a tug up as you do so.

incorrect The wrong buttock is being held, so when you push your hand backwards the result is a twist in the back rather than more length. Also, how can you extend the front leg when you are lifting the back one? Look at the spine on its gentle curve down to the floor, resulting in a floppy head. The hand on the floor is not important. Take your hand higher if you are inflexible, but keep your spine long and keep your body open.

alternative A helping hand is useful with this tricky posture. The reason for this angle is that it shows how the shoulders and hips should align. When they are aligned, the spine will be in a long line as opposed to bending up or curving down. Watch those front ribs as you twist, as they have a tendency to stick out. Closing them will allow you to feel that the back is long, and eliminate any hollow that may appear in the middle.

Balanced
postures

So what are the advantages of balancing on one leg? We are bipeds, with two legs and two hips providing our main means of movement, and any imbalance between them affects the whole body. By learning to balance on one foot, feeling your weight evenly on the foot through the ankle, both the knee and the hip are strengthened on that side. If both hips are kept even, then not only can hip imbalances be righted but all the torso and core muscles become involved.

Triangle Forward Bend

After all the work so far, you should really be feeling this in the legs. A Forward Bend is found in the hips, and the more they hinge forwards, the farther you will go forwards. Although not strictly a balance, this is a good neutral posture, linking naturally from twists to balances.

1 You have come up from the Revolved Triangle, so bend your knees in line with your toes, maintaining a lift in your tummy. Try not to stick your bottom out or to tuck it under. Use your thighs to hold you there and wait until they begin to burn.

2 Hinge forwards until your hands meet the floor and your chest is parallel to it. Your thighs should still be working. It is from these muscles that you slowly lift your bottom, lengthening the back of your legs. Keep your back long and your tummy pulled in.

3 Allow your upper body to relax. Feel the weight of the chest and head pull the lower spine long from the hips. The essence of a Forward Bend is to feel it within the backs of the legs. Let your head hang, while you push your seat bones up towards the ceiling.

incorrect The ability to touch the floor is worthy of praise, but not if it is achieved through back tension like this. Keep your back long by bending your knees and lifting your seat bones, or you will stretch the muscles of the back. (They are much smaller and tend to give way in the battle with the muscles in the backs of the legs.) Unlock your shoulders and use your thighs.

▶ **4** You can think of the head as a pendulum, hung from the hips via the spine, and here the picture gives a perfect example. Let the action of your heels pushing down and your buttocks going up leave your spine flowing down from your hips. Create as much space as you can between your legs and crotch for the hips to fold through as you bend over. Maintain the space in all your joints and enjoy letting your spine and hamstrings lengthen.

Flying Crow

Everyone falls over when they first try this posture, so you might as well resign yourself to the likelihood. If you are feeling brave but want some sort of soft landing, then practise in front of a cushion. Make sure you try it, for it is balance and not strength that is the key to the Flying Crow.

◀ 1 From the Triangle Forward Bend, bend the knees and start to raise the feet off the ground. If you feel that you have weak arms or are scared that you might fall flat on your face, then stay here. Lift up your heels and lift up your tummy. Your thighs will work hard but ignore them and concentrate on lifting your tummy so high that the legs begin to feel light. The more you lean forwards, the more you will find that the tummy pulls in.

▶ 2 A combination of leaning forwards to engage the stabilizing muscles of the back and a lot of tummy strength means that you can hang around in this posture for a while. The effort is felt in the tummy, but if the strength is not there you won't find yourself here. This is an example of balance through strength. It also shows you the lightness you should feel when performing the Flying Crow.

alternative 1 This picture shows a lower position in which more body weight is felt in the back of the arms. This will enable you to lift one foot tentatively off the floor. Make sure that you are looking forwards. This allows you to focus on the floor and reminds you of your balance. Pull your tummy in very tight as though it would lift straight through you. This will counter your impulse to collapse.

2 Once you find the balance point, the legs actually become quite light. This enables you to lift both legs up off the floor. Keep the shoulder blades open to make sure that both chest and back remain open. Lift your torso with your core strength at the same time – note the height of the tummy in this picture – rather than simply resting on your arms.

advanced If you keep lifting your tummy and the legs continue to be light, then you will find yourself in this position, the Handstand. Being upside down is so much fun and also very good for you. There are many reasons why inverting yourself may be good for you, but the best one is that it makes you feel like a child and reminds you of how much fun life can be. So even if you cannot suck yourself up to here by your tummy and back, then find a wall and play. If you do, remind yourself of how to keep your back open.

One-legged Biceps Curl

Balances are not easy, especially when you begin, because you feel as though something has been taken away from you. However, the mental and physical benefits you gain from their practice are far beyond the initial effort you may expend on learning them.

1 Having slowly rolled up to standing from Flying Crow, lift a leg and grab hold of the knee. Both hips and shoulders are even, although there is a great tendency to raise the hip and shoulder on the lifted side. Try and get the lovely long line in your collar bones.

▶ **2** One of the great things about yoga is the way it uses the body as its own personal gym machine. Here, you pull the knee high by using the biceps of the arms. As you do this, keep your shoulder blade wide and the elbow close to your side, as this will keep your shoulder blade flat to your ribs. This also has the effect of opening your chest. Notice that the head is right over the neck so that gravity goes straight through the body with the lowest possible resistance in the body.

incorrect Look how the leg is lifted by the top of the shoulder. This is intended to be a biceps curl, not a shrug and lift. Look how the hips are now uneven. If this happens to you, simply sit the raised sitting bone down and your hips will even out. Remember, balance is not just about remaining upright.

close-up This back view shows you how the action of curling your knee up can also teach you how to stabilize your shoulder blade. Keep your back broad and drop your shoulder blade so it feels as though that flat bone is curling under your armpit.

alternative If you really cannot balance in this posture, use a wall to steady yourself. Also, if you find that your hip is tight, then satisfy your need for knee height by stopping at parallel and concentrating on keeping your back long and upright. Pull your tummy in to help.

Karate Kid

This posture is a combination of strength and elegance, but at first it may feel ungainly and difficult. Try the easy version until you discover that your tummy and supporting hip take the strain, not the hip flexor of the lifted leg.

▶ **1** From One-legged Biceps Curl, lift your pubic bone up and lower your chest down to contract your tummy. Let go of the leg and pull your knee higher by pulling your tummy in harder. The effort should be in your tummy, not in your hip flexor. If you can find your balance here, drop your shoulder blades and lift your arms. You should feel the effort in the side of your waist and tummy. Let your supporting leg bend because that will help you to contact your middle. For the easy option stop at this point.

◀ **2** Look at the tummy – it is working hard to keep the leg up and straightened. The more you pull your tummy in, lift your pubic bone and lengthen your leg, the longer and higher the extension will be. If you lower your arms as here, it will give you a chance to engage your back. This will help you to stabilize yourself and also give you a feeling of pushing up and off something as you find a lift.

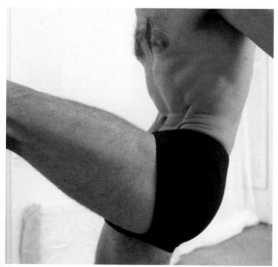

close-up This close-up explains the emphasis on the tummy in this posture. Look at the groove on the side of the waist. That's where you will find the core or support muscles you need as opposed to using the hip flexors, which have the tendency to tighten your hips when you rely on them too much. It also means that you are more likely to extend your leg higher, which will make you feel even more graceful.

incorrect This method of Karate Kid is guaranteed to have your hip flexors flexing, since the entire weight of your leg is being held by them. Notice how the tummy is bulging. As a result of that bulge, the lower spine is once again called upon to hold up the body all by itself. Notice also how the lean backwards is preventing the tummy from being pulled in.

alternative As with the One-legged Biceps Curl, if you feel your balance is something to be worked on, use a wall to steady yourself. As you do so, use your other hand to feel how hard the hip flexor of the lifted leg is working (it will pop up like a cable). With your best endeavour, make your tummy pull in even harder. You may find that your leg will lift even higher as a result.

Seated Eagle

This posture is excellent for your insides, since they are flushed with blood in the action of squeezing your thighs together. After you have finished this posture, let yourself unwrap into the Tree, as you will now find it quite easy to balance and it helps to strengthen the hip further.

◀ **1** Bend the right knee, and cross the left leg over and tuck the toes behind. Cross the right arm over the left at the elbows, aiming the palms together. Push your elbows away from you and up to keep some space between your arms and your chest if you can. Keep the hips level and balanced.

▶ **2** To release the body, pull your tummy up and in, balancing on the straight leg. Unwrap your arms and drop your shoulder blades to lift them up. Place the previously crossing leg into a right angle to form a classic yoga shape, the Tree.

close-up It is not clear where the name Seated Eagle originated, but it does makes sense. You are "sitting" cross-legged, and the pretzel-like action of the arms opens your back and flares your shoulder blades – to spread your wings. The body should sit directly over your hips. Notice the light between the arms – try to keep the elbows up and the hands away from the body.

incorrect This is almost a "Seated Buzzard", with the curve in the middle and the hump in the back! If you collapse your middle and lean forwards, the head will still try to give you the impression that you are upright. Copy this and you will not feel the work of the posture in your thigh but feel as though you resemble a clumsy knot. Spread your wings and sit up. Don't slump.

alternative If you feel unsteady, then place your hands on your thighs and use your arms to help hold your spine long. Use the simplicity of this posture to keep your hips even and feel the work in your thigh.

Rocket Man

Practise this posture, taking time to repeat each leg, as through regular practice you will attain a good awareness of your hips, tummy and back. Also, through learning the feelings you gain in your body and replicating them into other postures, you will gain stability and understanding.

1 Balancing on one leg, use your arms to help stabilize your body on your bent supporting knee. Keep your shoulders down away from your ears and really extend backwards with your back leg. Think about lengthening your hip and thigh, as this will help you to feel the stretch from your stomach to your toes.

2 Notice that the chest is slightly above the hips. This allows the back to pull together, making it solid. The tummy is also pulled up to help stabilize the lower back. This also helps to steady the hip of the supporting leg. Really extend through your back leg as though you are pushing off to rocket forwards.

close-up You could call this posture "T", because ideally that is what it should look like. Keep your shoulders open away from your head and you should feel the muscles in the back engage to give you the lift you are looking for. Notice how the front ribs are closed to allow the spine to stretch its full length. The tummy is drawn in tight to support the lower spine and to help extend the back leg and open the hip. Try it, keeping your hips even.

incorrect More "Droopy" than Rocket, this is a common error. The mushroom back means the hips are the highest point, so the disengaged muscles lining the spine are working too hard. Push your back leg straight and lift your chest.

▶ **3** This is an enjoyable posture and this picture explains why. In Rocket Man you feel as though you are flying, with so much lightness in the hips that the supporting leg almost disappears. The body feels very long because of the simultaneous extension of the back leg backwards and the chest forwards. All the time the tummy is lifting up to let you feel a lightness, and the entire body begins to open. From here anything seems possible. Find your lightness and fly, even if you cheat by keeping one foot on the floor.

Seated
postures

When you get to the floor section you will need to remember not to collapse. Although a greater proportion of you rests on the floor, the increase in sensory response provided can give you even more of an idea of where your core is and how you lift. Always come to the floor exercises fresh. Feel your seat bones on the floor and lift your body up from them. Allow the hips to hinge; do not collapse them and bend from the spine. Most of all, remember that any Forward Bend comes from the hips, regardless of the length of the legs.

Seated Forward Bend

You either love this posture or the back of your body complains so loudly that you don't. Be patient. Remember that the body must hinge in the middle, with both sides of the hinge as long as possible. To lie flat, the entire back of the body must be open.

▶ **1** Let your head relax so that your neck is long, and make your tummy as long as possible. After all, the longer the tummy, the longer your lower spine, and that means the deeper you hinge forwards. Think of lengthening your lower spine out of your hips, as opposed to dragging yourself forwards with your arms, and you'll find that any injury is very unlikely. You will also begin to understand more this feeling of a hinge. If you get the chance, ask someone to give you a push there. It's quite safe and feels lovely.

◀ **2** When you can, let the head bow and relax, as you did in the standing Forward Bend. Once again, you should feel that your spine is lengthening up, out and away from your hips. Extend your arms, relax and take time to breathe.

incorrect When people madly grab at their feet to show that they can touch their toes, it sometimes seems that if they let go, they would ping backwards owing to all the tension in their bowed spines. This posture is great as a back stretch, but as a Forward Bend not much of the body is going forwards and there is a big bend in the back. Since we spend so much time slouching over work, dinner or watching television, take this time to extend your spine and lengthen the backs of your legs.

alternative If you are not flexible, try this version and lift your chest as high up your thighs as possible. You will find a stretch in the back of your legs, even if your knees are as bent as you see here. Note how the length of the spine is mirrored by the length in the back of the thighs. Stay here, feeling the freedom of your spine and the stretch in your hips and hamstrings. Only when these lifting muscles are strong enough to counter the tightness in your legs will your hamstrings truly soften.

Table

Have you ever seen a deck chair on a windy day, when its seat is blown through the frame? The Table should eventually have a similar feel, where the back muscles are "blowing" the front muscles open and up. Use your hands and feet to feel the floor and find the "lift".

◄ **1** The Table feels like a natural progression from a Seated Forward Bend, since all that opening needs consolidating. So sit up. Place your hands behind your bottom, slightly wider than shoulder width, which makes it easier to find your back strength until the flexibility of your shoulders appears. As you push up, keep your elbows soft and try to get your chest higher than your shoulders. Try to lengthen the front of your body, and you should find this helps to provide some more strength to stay up. If you find that dropping your head back all the way is difficult, either open your jaw wide or lengthen the back of your neck.

▶ **2** The Table is similar to the Side Triangle, in that you should feel as if you are making a tunnel underneath you. This means really having to find the muscles of your back, especially those that draw the shoulder blades down the back. When you find these, you will feel that they are responsible for lifting the chest higher and higher, opening the front of the shoulders and chest. So find the floor, push up and make a tunnel.

close-up The feet are the forgotten part of this posture – use them and they will help. If you have inflexible ankles, then really extend your toes to the floor, and not only will your ankles open but your arches will also improve. The more you can push down with your feet, the more you can engage the backs of the legs to help you lift. After all, they've been lengthened in the previous posture and now it is their chance to be strengthened in this one. Use your feet and feel the floor.

incorrect People execute this style of Table when they are unaware of their backs and of the fact that they have legs they can stretch. How many times when you've been slouched over your work do you push your chest up to release the tension you feel in it? Well this posture is exactly the same feeling. Get a neck, stop slouching, and you will understand how refreshed you can feel when you come down from the Table.

close-up Try not to lock your elbows, since this hyperextends them and takes the weight out of the muscles in the back and into your joints. If you can, keep working on getting your shoulder blades flat to your ribs, as this will really help to open your shoulders.

Cobbler

This posture is also known as the Butterfly Hinge. Look at how the legs have opened right up, like wings. There is a lightness within the hips that allows this. Open the hips and revisit these postures as many times as necessary, to enable you to find this lightness in their separation.

1 Sit down from the Table and bring your heels towards your bottom as far as is comfortable. Holding your feet or ankles for support, lift your pubic bone up and try not to lean backwards. The higher you lift, the more your knees will spread apart.

2 From rolling back, pull your tummy up and in to lift you upright. As you do this, keep the feeling of separating the knees within your hips. These are separate and distinct sensations that do not seem to fit together, but practice will show that they do.

▶ **4** It may take a very long time for your hips to open sufficiently to allow your head to reach the floor, but wherever you get to in leaning forwards, remember that the more open your hips, the more space you have to roll forwards and through. Spend time getting your knees towards the floor before worrying yourself over how far you are from the floor. Spread your knees and hinge from the hips and your spine will look after itself.

3 If your inner thighs will not give in, use your arms to help maintain the length of your spine. Pulling the tummy up and in helps in two ways. It stops the lower spine collapsing and, second, the more you lift up, the more likely you will be able to release your inner thighs.

incorrect Look at the tension within the upper back during the struggle to get over the hips. As a result of this battle the inner thighs join in, resulting in the knees going up not down. This posture will only push tightness to where tightness already exists. Be alive and be intelligent. Feel the lift and begin to experience the opening of your body.

Bridge

Think of the arc beneath a bridge – the smoother the arc, the stronger the structure. So when you attempt this posture, remember to keep as long an arc as possible in your back. This will prevent you from putting the bend on one part of the back, which always leads to discomfort.

1 From the Cobbler, lift your pubic bone up between your legs, and you'll find you begin to roll backwards. As your lower spine begins to near the floor, your legs will feel light enough to bring them into parallel lines with a nice bend in the knees. Keep lifting your pubic bone up to roll you down, and, as your spine unrolls on the floor, bring your heels as close to your bottom as is comfortable.

2 Once on the floor, lay your hands on either side of your body, pushing your forearms and hands down. This will help you to feel the muscles between your shoulder blades. Then press your heels down to feel the floor and keep rolling your pubic bone up between your legs. The thighs will feel the major work. If they don't, the lack of pubic lift will mean your lower back will begin to constrict.

3 If the posture in step 2 is very comfortable, then continue to lift your shoulder blades up off the floor and lift your pubic bone up between your legs. If in this higher posture you feel light, then take your right hand under your right shoulder and your left under your left. Stay here. Do not push with your arms. Keep lifting your middle, with the power in your thighs and the lift in your hips.

close-up This angle is visually how you should feel. Just as in a standing Forward Bend, your hips are highest. Your thighs and hips are your strength. If you lift from them, you will find far less constriction in your back than if you struggle to lift with your arms. This entire sequence of photographs is one long roll of the pubic bone up between the legs.

▶4 The Bridge or the Big Back Bend has a status much the same as the Forward Bend or Handstand within a yoga class, for it shows everyone you have a flexible back. Try to think about being upside down, as if you have been walking on your hands and feet and a giant has turned you the wrong way up. This will make you feel as though you are pushing up not just with your arms but your legs and tummy as well. If you can play in this posture, move and sway. Try picking limbs up from the floor to reaffirm where your lift comes from. You are upside down, so be light-hearted and play.

Double Pigeon

The mechanics of this pose make it quite hard to strain and push, so in order to understand why this posture is so important, stay in it, rest in it and work intelligently within it. Be gentle with your body as, even though this posture feels lovely, going into it can elicit some strong feelings.

1 The action of placing one shin upon the other will, for some, be beyond the accommodation of their hips but if the shin does lie almost flat, then trust in your tummy strength and the hip will open up. As you sit there, sit as tall out of your hips as is possible.

2 Push your top knee down (in the Assembly position, both knees) and lift your pubic bone between your legs. You will feel the tummy pull in and the knees spread. Do not lean backwards, just roll your hips up and back. Stay here and feel the spread in the legs.

alternative If when you try and place your shin on top of the other, your body prevents your leg from moving or the knee sticks up high in the air, or your ankle and foot feel as though they are going to snap, then move into the Assembly position sitting with simple crossed-legs.

▶ **3** Keep sucking your tummy in and up until you feel your hips begin to roll forwards. Keep rolling them forwards, up and over your legs, until you find yourself over your legs. Push your bottom down and back, pull your tummy in and up and lift your chest up by using the muscles of your upper back. This will extend your spine and allow you to find space within your hips and lower spine.

advanced If your hips do not feel the desired deep stretch with your shins lying on each other, then pull your knees so that they are inside your ankles and you will find the depth of sensation you have been looking for. Breathe slowly and deeply, emphasizing the exhale to help you let go of the tension in those deep muscles.

Batfink

In this posture you wrap your arms around your legs as though you were cloaking them in bat wings. This will keep your back open and broad while you curl your pubic bone up and draw your knees to your chest by pulling your tummy away from your thighs.

▶ **1** Start by balancing on your bottom and, while maintaining your balance, learn to curl your pubic bone up and your tail between your legs, as this is the beginning of extending your spine into a long, smooth "C" shape. You have to hold this "C" shape in order to have a smooth roll from bottom to shoulders and back up again. Let your arms go forwards and your chest backwards since this will help you round and open your upper spine. You do not want to throw yourself up and down with the momentum from your legs, so spend some time here until you feel that you have the smoothest "C" back you can possibly get.

◀ **2** Rolling back and up is fun. You get a lovely feeling of massaging the muscles along your back and the impression that you are a child's toy. The art of rolling back and up lies in your pubic lift, as this will keep any gaps or holes in your spine from appearing, in other words, any part of your back that does not wish to roll with the rest of your back on the floor. Notice how the body is still in exactly the same position even though it has been turned on to the space between the shoulder blades.

advanced If you have rolled back and forth quite happily and fancy a challenge, try recreating a Forward Bend while balancing on your bottom. Enter Batfink as in step 1, then slowly pull your bent knees as close to your shoulders as you can. Lift the arms and straighten your legs by using the muscles in the front of your thighs. Try it out. Play one leg at a time.

alternative If there is no way your spine will allow you to roll back and forth, assume this position. Keep lifting your pubic bone into your tummy, while keeping the knees relaxed above your hips. This will strengthen your abdomen and allow you eventually to roll through the hips.

incorrect Look here at how the chest is lifted and the tummy is forced to bulge out, leaving more weight to be carried in the lower back. Also, the hip flexors are the main muscle holding the knees high. When these tighten they pull the hip girdle forwards with them and, since your hips are attached to your spine, this means a more pronounced hollow in your lower back. Don't allow feeling tall in the posture to come at the expense of being tight. Besides, straight lines don't roll.

Tortoise

Achieving this posture takes patience and time. When inside it at your limit, slow down and take time. Come out as if coming out of hibernation, for if you move quickly, you will miss great subtleties and sensations. The Tortoise can unlock the deep places where we store our tension.

▶ **1** The Tortoise posture is all about coming forwards. Just as a tortoise extends its head out of its protective shell, you have to figure out how to pull your body up and forwards out of your hips. Put your arms under your bent legs and extend forwards. The posture demonstrated here is more than deep enough for most people, since it requires you not only to roll your hips forwards between your legs but also to extend your spine forwards and up from your rolled hips. The result is ~~~~~~~~~~~~~ in the hips and lower spine.

◀ **2** This is a real challenge since both your legs and your body have to go forwards away from your hips. The arms extend backwards, away from the head. This is going beyond the Forward Bend you are used to, since you have to take your body beneath your legs. However, remember that the bend originates inside the hips, not through dragging your spine between your legs. Whatever you do, keep your back long and take time to feel the groin open up to give the hips space to move through.

incorrect A classic posture of the head bound student, this method of performing the Tortoise will inevitably end with you on your back. The body is collapsing forwards, beginning with the shoulders and moving all the way down the back. Although the hips may feel the stretch, they will not stretch far because of the distinct lack of support from the rest of the body. Be patient and you will win in the end.

alternative If your hips allow for very little play, follow this example. Use your arms as struts to help lengthen and lift your spine up and out of your hips. Not only will this feel more comfortable, but it will also put you in touch with the tummy lift. This lift, when strong enough, will allow your muscles around the hip joint to soften so that the hips can then hinge closer to the thighs. If you find yourself here, then you need to pay more attention to all the Forward Bend exercises.

advanced If your hips and spine allow, proceed forwards and down, rolling your palms up to the ceiling (thumbs facing in) so you can try to grab hold of your bottom or clasp hands. The idea is that through slotting your shoulder blades under your knees, the knees can act as a weight to push your body lower. Clasping the hands on the lower spine then provides some sensations you can respond to and lift away from. Extend your body as long as you can along the floor and you will feel all the tension release from your tail.

Shoulder Stand

There are many benefits to practising inverted postures, primarily because it flushes the head and neck with a large supply of blood. This not only helps to relax you and release tension from your head and neck, but may also leave you feeling clearer and fresher than when you began.

1 Lift your pubic bone up into your tummy until your legs are rolling over your head. Lift your shoulder blades up off the floor. Any neck pain should disappear when you work the back muscles hard to lift the shoulder blades up off the floor.

2 If resting your knees on your head strains your back, try this version, as it demands a long spine. Basic rules: if your neck hurts, then lift your shoulder blades up off the floor. If your spine or lower back hurts, then take your hips backwards away from your head.

alternative Roll backwards into an "L". Bend the knees as you need to. Pull the abdomen in, brace the floor with your arms and draw your shoulder blades down your body away from your ears. Menstruating women will benefit from staying in this posture. If you really want to relax then put your legs up against a wall.

advanced Attempt this posture only if you are fully aware of your tummy and back core muscles. If you are, then you will find it. If not, don't try it. It is fun and the key is found between your shoulder blades.

▶**3** Follow the same two rules. If your neck hurts and feels tight, lift your shoulder blades up and away from the floor. (Persistent pain means don't be silly, stop doing it and seek advice.) Second, if your lower spine aches, then take your hips back away from your head. Then warm your kidneys with your hands and stay there, constantly feeling the lift, for as long as you feel comfortable. There are many benefits, so practise and learn to feel them. Please note that women are not advised to practise inverted postures during the first three days of menstruation.

Fish to Corpse

These three postures flow into each other and lead you into a deeper state of relaxation. The Fish helps you extend and open the front of your body. The Baby pose helps you be aware of the expansion of your spine and the freedom of your hips. Corpse lets you become aware of this space.

◀ **1 fish** This a classic counter pose to end with after a Shoulder Stand. The reason why can be seen in the neck. Having compressed the front of the neck and lengthened the back, the pushing of the elbows down and the arching of the upper back can allow you to drop your head right back until the top of your head rests on the floor. Remember to stretch your legs and lengthen your tummy, so that you feel as though the arch in the top of your body is grounded in the rest of it. As you do this, try not to make the arch come solely from your lower spine, as this may make your back ache when you slowly lower yourself down. Most of all, open your chest. Breathe into the space between your shoulder blades and, as you breathe out, lengthen your waist.

▶ **close-up** This angle shows the positioning of the hands and that the emphasis is most certainly found in lifting and opening the chest. See if you can find out how to arch your upper back without having to overarch your lower back. Breathe deeply into the top of your chest and open the space between your shoulders.

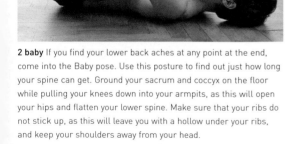

2 baby If you find your lower back aches at any point at the end, come into the Baby pose. Use this posture to find out just how long your spine can get. Ground your sacrum and coccyx on the floor while pulling your knees down into your armpits, as this will open your hips and flatten your lower spine. Make sure that your ribs do not stick up, as this will leave you with a hollow under your ribs, and keep your shoulders away from your head.

3 From the Baby you know it is time to relax, so lower both heels to the floor with a bend in the knees. This should make sure that your spine feels long and flat on the floor.

4 Let one leg go straight, but as you do so, notice how much of your spine pulls up and off the floor. This is owing to tension in the front of your hip. Allow your leg to let go and the spine to remain soft.

5 corpse When you feel ready, allow your other leg to go straight and, once again, watch how the spine lifts. If your lower spine hurts with both legs down, then return to both legs bent and heels on the floor. Let go and be prepared to spend some time here.

Chilling Out

There is no question that when you're tired you want to rest and that after resting you'll feel better. Another simple fact is that when your muscles are relaxed, you tend to feel relaxed in your head too. When you have finished your practice, you may well find that you feel tired.

◀ 1 Try lying on your front with the soft parts of your body on the floor. You'll discover that it is very easy to find this sinking feeling when there are no bony parts of you causing discomfort. We come back to the scientific law that states that for each action, there is an equal and opposite reaction. So, the harder you work, the better you'll rest. When you know just where the tired muscles are, it is easier to relax them. Equally, the harder they work, the easier it is to get them to relax. What you end up with is a body ready and willing to relax. If you repeat this regularly, you will learn to know the feeling of letting go. Eventually this awareness will be with you all the time, not just after exercise.

▶ 2 Roll on to your back and keep that feeling of sinking that you found on your tummy and let your body go "splat", including your bony parts. Check your hips are open and your shoulder blades are broad and allow your chest to open. Let go, it's the end.

3 As you lie there, you will want to think and be active in your head. So get as far away from your head as you can by finding and mentally feeling your feet with your consciousness. Physically do nothing and mentally take a holiday to your toes. Your mind will want you to fidget, move, think or imagine. It will cling madly on to any source of entertainment, even down to counting your breathing or heart rate.

4 Against the wandering mind, you have an advantage. You have your body beneath you, with its many thousands of impulses and sensations. If your mind wants to be busy, entertain it by watching, living, the sensations of you. This is true relaxation, meditation, chilling out – whatever you want to call it. But most of all, the beauty is that everything you've been wanting – release, a source of wellbeing – is you. Let go and feel.

Sequences

There are three warm-up sequences here, and four routines. You do not need to copy everything you see, but practise what you can. If you like, refer back to the main page for each posture for more details. Spend time in each of the postures to see how your breathing affects them, or flow between them with only one breath held in each. Try spending at least ten breaths in each posture in one practice and then only one in another, as this will build endurance and cardio-vascular fitness respectively. At the end of each sequence, make time for five minutes of stillness.

Putting It Together

Look at a river and you will see that in the middle its current runs fast, taking all the sediment it carries far down towards the sea. Look now at the sides or the banks of the river and you will see the current moving slower, eddying and playing with the sediment it carries and laying it down on the banks. This build-up of deposits will eventually lead to a change in the shape of the river as it begins to push the fast-flowing centre farther and farther away from it.

Fat, the river and you

Your body is one big river of energy. Wherever there is poor circulation, sediment (or fat) will build up, and when it does, not only the inside but also the outside will show this. If you sit down, remaining static and inactive, it is common sense that you will not feel or look in prime physical condition. After all, your muscles, which act as pumps, are not active to help your river keep flowing freely inside you, and build-up will occur.

To help you find your river and help activate these natural pumps, put together all that you've learnt so far: hinging through your hips from ape to man to find the "pumps" in your buttocks and thighs, using your back and tummy to keep your spine long and free.

Think of all you learn and read in here as a map. But make sure that at every stage you ask yourself "Does this map make sense to me?" If it doesn't, don't hesitate to discard it and start again. If it does make sense, then follow and feel so you find these words, actions, postures and descriptions making sense in your body. Listen and feel until they become a physical sensation.

Warming up

On the following pages are some simple warm-up sequences. All of them are flowing, which means no postures are held for long; they simply flow as the breath does, from inhale to exhale, standing to bending, looking up to stepping back. All the time you are doing them, make sure that your spine is long, your tummy is engaged and your neck is soft from the shoulder blades going down and out, not up and in.

If you can't do this, return to the beginning and relearn where your core strength is. Remember, too, that you don't move just during the 10 or 15 minutes of this routine, so why apply these rules only for the duration of your practice? When you drive a car, are your shoulder blades up around your ears because of stress? If so, get them down. When you are standing at the sink or cooking, is your spine long and your tummy pulled in to support your lower spine? When you sit at your office desk, can you find the lift up and off the chair? If you become more aware, you will find that all movement will begin to feel easier.

left and right The exercises here can teach you to find your core strength and the lunges and standing postures will help increase your stamina. However, you need to put this information to good use in the rest of your life as well, not just when you are being "fit", and then you will really feel it.

Relaxing Sequence – Warm-up 1

This is a relaxing warm-up to try before moving on to the later postures. This way, the muscles will be primed and know what to expect, lessening the chance of injury. These movements are intended to flow, one into the other, so don't hold each one for long, maybe 30 seconds or two

1 lying down Begin by lying on your back with your arms at your sides. Use your senses to discover how much of you rests flat on the floor, and every time you exhale see if you can release down a little more.

2 upper back arch As you breathe in, direct your breath to the top part of your chest and see if through contracting your upper back – the muscles that line the spine in between your shoulder blades – you are able to lift up your breastbone.

3 softened chest As you breathe out, soften your chest so that the upper back arch is allowed to soften. Repeat these actions so that your upper back begins to be more mobile. See if you can feel just your upper back moving.

7 both knees to chest Slowly pull both knees to your chest. Drag your heels to your bottom before you lift your legs, as this will allow you to maintain a stable core, as opposed to your back having to arch or your abdomen bulge.

8 letter "L" The straightness of your legs is secondary to the feeling of work in your core and stability in your hips. It doesn't matter whether your legs are straight; keep your back long along the floor. Feel as though you are stretching the back of your body. Breathe and lengthen your body.

9 lowering the legs Begin lowering both legs by bending and separating your knees, while simultaneously lifting your pubic bone. This will mean that you are using primarily your core strength to lower your legs.

deep breaths. The whole sequence will take only a few minutes, but the benefits of doing it regularly will soon show in the way that your core strength is improved, and all kinds of movements, not just the ones in this book, will become easier.

4 knee up to chest After resting for a few moments, exhale deeply. Lift one leg up into your chest, clasping your hands just below your knee. Keep both sides of your waist long and see if you can lengthen your buttocks and lower spine.

5 submarine Let go of the knee and extend your leg. If your leg cannot straighten, then keep your knee bent and push your heel high. The key here is not to let your tummy bulge up and your lower back arch off the floor. Keep pulling your ribs and stomach away from the upright leg.

6 lowering the leg Lower the leg with a bend in the knee and the leg slightly turned out, or straight. Maintain the strength in your tummy so that neither your back arches nor your tummy bulges up. Repeat with the other leg.

10 roll up Once your feet have reached the floor, allow your legs to roll away from each other fully and pull your tummy up and in so hard that you end up looking through your legs. Follow this pull and roll up to sitting.

11 roll over Be aware of the movement of your hips as you roll up. As you roll over your legs, do so with your hips and not simply by leaning forwards from your lower spine. Learn to hinge forwards, so repeat rolling back and forth until you can really feel the movement of your hips.

12 corpse Finally, roll back, doing so along your entire spine. When on the floor, slowly extend one leg, then the other, and rest. Use your senses to see if any more of your body is resting on the floor than when you began.

Resting Rocket Man – Warm-up 2

This sequence is all based upon activity and release, so when being active, really use your muscles to make you feel as though you are flying through the poses. Then, when you enter the Child poses they will feel like home since your muscles will be crying out for some rest and this will help

1 lying on front Lie down on your front and concentrate on the soft parts of your body on the floor (tummy, thighs and chest). Try to relax until you feel as though as much as possible of the front of you is touching the floor.

2 chest lift Pull your tummy as far up and off the floor as possible to keep your lower spine in place and lengthen the front of your body from your chest to your forehead. Keep your shoulder blades open and arms relaxed, as they were in the previous posture.

3 grounded rocket man Keeping the back of your neck long, your tummy up and your legs relaxed, lift your elbows up until your thumbs meet the creases under your buttocks. Make sure you leave your shoulder blades open.

7 double leg lift To lift both legs is tricky without drooping your lower spine or collapsing your chest, so pay attention to those details as opposed to the height of your legs off the floor.

8 big-belly child Again, use your abdomen to stop your back collapsing as you push yourself back. The wider your knees, the more open your hips will feel, but if your lower back feels tight, try belly gazing which will help to free any tension.

9 elbows Resting your head on your thumbs, keep your navel the highest point underneath you. Make a long, smooth arc from head to toe to let the strength of your front open your back.

you let your muscles relax further into the pose. Since it does not take long, try repeating it until your body seems to flow through the sequence with your muscles smoothly taking you from one pose to the next. Repeated regularly, you will really start to feel the benefits in your core strength.

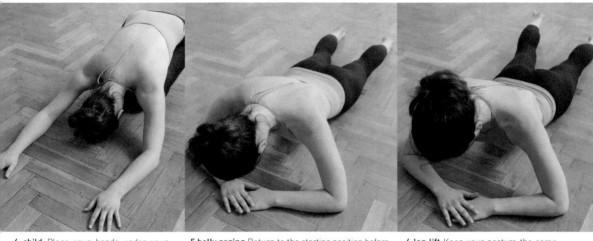

4 child Place your hands under your shoulders and pull your tummy firmly up and in. This will brace your back as you push your bottom towards your heels. If your shoulders are very tight, take your arms into a wide "Y".

5 belly gazing Return to the starting position before finding this pose and see if you are any more relaxed than before. Then, placing your hands beneath your forehead, push your elbows down and gaze down at your abdomen, feeling it pull up and in.

6 leg lift Keep your posture the same: open back, long and lifted front, long lower spine. Lift one leg by lengthening your thigh back and away from you. Remember to try squeezing the top of that leg's buttock. Change legs.

10 naughty child This encourages you to push your bottom in the air. Think of a long arch from your bottom to your fingertips – let the length in the back reflect the length of your front.

11 press up Ideally your shoulders are directly over your wrists, with a big space beneath you. Push your chest up off the floor to open the space between your shoulder blades and once again find the arc from your forehead to your toes.

12 lying on front See how far you can let go into the floor; how much more of your front touches the floor than when you began. Consciously contract a group of muscles, then release and relax them.

Standing Sequence – Warm-up 3

This warm-up allows you to take all that you have learnt about your body so far and apply it to a standing stance. We spend most of our waking life in an upright posture, so it makes sense that we practise something that mimics the patterns of our everyday life or we stand little chance of

1 standing Stand tall with your chest lifted, hands by the sides, and as you stand, feel the connection from the heels to the back of your head. Draw the shoulder blades out and down. Soften the chest as you exhale.

2 lifting arms Inhale. Feel the connection between your arms and your back and lift the arms as you drop the shoulder blades, so the shoulders are relaxed and down. Take the arms forward, so you can feel the movement of the shoulder blades, then bring both arms above your head.

3 forward bend Exhale. Soften your knees and lift the bottom so you can lengthen the abdomen and spine. This will ensure that you hinge forwards from the hips, rather than collapse through the lower spine.

7 single leg stretch Exhale. Use your hips as a hinge to simultaneously push the front leg long and lower the torso over the front leg. Enjoy the stretch but keep some softness in your front knee. Do not hyperextend your knee.

8 looking up forward bend Inhale. Step forwards, placing your feet together. Try to do this by bending your back leg. As you step you will really feel the hip of the straight leg. See if you can keep some lightness in your body as you make this move. You may have to make two smaller steps.

9 forward bend Exhale. Push your heels down, keeping the knees soft, lift the bottom, pull the tummy up in and let the head relax and drop down to the feet. Place your palms flat on the floor either side of your feet.

changing our habitual patterns of movement. Perform this warm-up until it makes sense, and you can really let your breath take you from one posture to the next. When you have achieved this, try to discover a feeling of light-footedness, so that when you move you are in full control.

4 looking up forward bend Inhale. Using your upper back rather than the neck, look up and open the ribs so that you will have more room to inhale. Lengthen the stomach and keep lifting your bottom to the ceiling.

5 lunge Exhale. Keeping your front leg bent at 90 degrees, lunge the other leg backwards, really concentrating on lengthening your leg right up through the abdomen. Keep the hips above the level of the knees, meanwhile keeping the muscles of the stomach strong.

6 lunge Inhale. Raise your hands over the head. Lift up through the hips and keep the lower spine long by lifting your pubic bone. Keep the back leg long and straight, and feel the sensations happening in your hips.

10 flat back to lifting arms Inhale. Look up and extend your spine. Soften the knees and pull the tummy in, so you can hinge up to standing through your hips while maintaining a long spine. Drop the shoulders to lift the arms.

11 standing Exhale. Relax your chest as you breath out, so you feel the weight of your arms between the shoulder blades. Remember to take your arms in front of the body to keep the shoulder blades flat to the ribs. Repeat on the other side to make one round of this sequence.

Earthing Sequence

When you are tired, stressed or anxious, getting close to the floor and truly feeling it can allow your breath and emotions to calm down. Use this sequence to learn where the floor is and how you tense muscles unnecessarily while performing the simplest of postures.

1 sleeping superman Lie on the floor and try to feel yourself free-falling through the floor. Play with the upper back and shoulder blades. This will help you to feel the back open up.

2 child Breathe and take your time. Use the tummy and back to help you move between this and the posture in the previous picture.

3 cobbler Push yourself all the way back on to your bottom. Keep the hips low and feel the buttocks stretch. Use these muscles to help to separate your knees.

7 knee hug Lower your hips slowly so that you know where the weight of the body is. Keep your awareness in the hips as you hug the knees. Lengthen the lower spine.

8 single leg "L" Lay one leg flat, really stretching through the hip as you lengthen the other leg towards the ceiling. Keep the weight inside the hips. Relax the chest and keep the tummy in.

9 single knee hug As you bend the knee in the air, feel the buttocks and your lower spine lengthen. Do not lose this sensation, but really savour it. Repeat on the other side from single leg "L".

4 letter "L" Squeeze your buttocks to open the legs, then lift the pubic bone to help you roll along the spine to form the shape of the letter "L". If you are inflexible, you may find it necessary to bend your knees.

5 batfink Hold on to the back of the knees to help you begin rolling and make sure you roll through all of the spine, without holes or bumps.

6 bridge Roll up to Cobbler and then, with your feet ready, roll the spine down and lift the hips up in the air. Keep the work in the hips so the spine stays long.

10 upper back bow Lower both legs to the floor, keeping the weight of them inside the hips and abdomen so that the lower back stays long. Separate the shoulders and lengthen the upper spine along the floor.

11 upper back arch Soften your chest and contract the shoulders down and out to feel the neck lengthen and the middle and upper back arch.

12 corpse Release and relax the muscles you have just worked. Feel them soften into the floor and, once again, try to free-fall through the floor. Let the earth hold you up.

Energizing Sequence

To energize, you have to get everything moving, so this sequence is composed of big postures requiring large movements to flow between them. Within the space of these movements you can really begin to feel the body beneath you. Take your time getting from one posture to the next.

1 lunge After performing up to five single leg lunges, stay in the Lunge and really push the back leg straight. Keep the work in the hips by lifting the tummy.

2 pert buttocked warrior Roll the hip of the back leg around, while keeping the front knee still. Let the arms drop to shoulder height, but keep their weight in between the shoulder blades.

3 triangle Push the front leg straight and use that hip as a hinge to rotate the torso towards the ground. Use the tummy to keep the chest and hips rolled at an angle of 90 degrees to the floor.

7 forward bend When you have completed the postures on both sides, jump forwards and, with soft knees, push the heels down while at the same time lifting the bottom.

8 karate kid Roll up to standing and bring your beginning lunge leg with you. Contract the tummy backwards, so that you feel the weight of the leg in the stomach muscles.

9 rocket man Take that leg backwards in line with your body and really stretch that leg through the sensations you felt in Rocket Man.

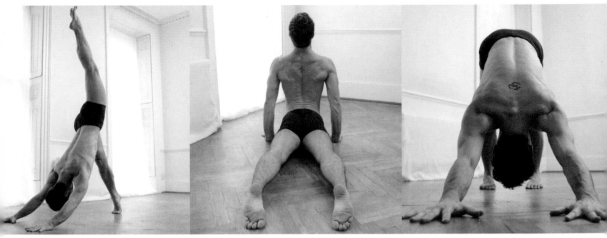

4 dog split Use the tummy and back hip to roll the chest parallel to the floor. Pushing your hands flat, kick the back leg straight behind you so it makes a line with the wrist.

5 up dog Slowly lower yourself into the Press Up position and, with both feet on the floor, drop the hips and lift the chest. Use the back, keep it open and draw the shoulders down.

6 down dog Lift back into Press Up position from your tummy. Continue to lift the tummy as you separate the shoulders while pushing the bottom back and up. Lunge the other leg forwards and repeat.

10 thigh lunge Bend the supporting knee and stretch your back, lowering yourself into this knee trembling pose. Make sure you keep the abdomen high, off the front thigh.

11 revolved triangle Take the opposite hand alongside the front foot and lift the bottom up with the other hand. This will twist you towards the leg, but use the tummy to help twist you around. Via Press Up, Up Dog, Down Dog and a Jump, go back to Rocket Man on the other leg.

12 triangle forward bend Finish with another Press Up, Up Dog and Down Dog sequence, and then jump straight into this posture. Keep the knees soft and lift the bottom. Finish with some relaxing postures and stillness.

Strength Sequence

Although this sequence seems to rely on arm strength, the strength you need is in fact to be found in your core. When you begin the first posture, try to feel the weight of your body being carried within your back and stomach, rather than in your shoulders and arms.

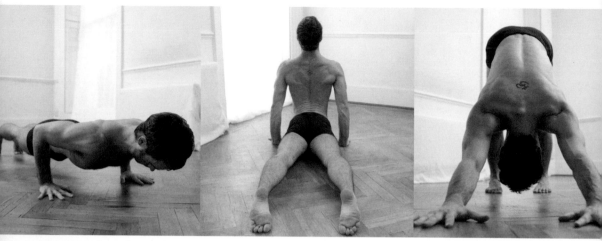

1 press up Keep the navel high underneath you and draw the shoulder blades down the back. Then bend the elbows (do not collapse) and, as you exhale, relax the chest so that your full weight is felt in the back.

2 up dog Drop your hips and lift the chest with the muscles you used in the Press Up. Stretch the legs through the tummy back to the toes.

3 down dog Using your tummy and stopping briefly in top Press Up, lift the hips into Down Dog. Pay careful attention to the feelings in the wrists, shoulders and tummy.

7 side triangle Roll on to the outside of the back foot and roll on to your side, so the top leg remains in the air. See if you can grab hold of that top big toe without crushing the space underneath you.

8 jump Jump into Lunge on the other side and repeat from the Lunge to the Dog Split and Side Triangle on the other side. Then, after completing both sides, jump both feet to behind the wrists, drop your head and lift your bottom. Release any tension from your lower spine.

9 triangle forward bend Feel the tummy pull up and in as you lift your bottom. Pay attention to this lift.

4 jump Having felt the strength through your wrists, shoulders and tummy, keep it strong as you jump up. At the top of the jump, take one foot forward, ready for the Lunge.

5 lunge Keep light in this posture, as if you are still in the top of the Jump. Use the back to hold the arms up and the tummy to hold you buoyant from the hips.

6 dog split In one smooth move, push the front leg all the way back in a Dog Split, but keep the shoulders and hips even to maintain the strength of the posture in your core.

10 flying crow Place your knees on the back of the arms, lift the heels and find that lift. It feels as though a rope around your waist is holding you up.

11 handstand (advanced flying crow) Press your hands down, contract the back and let the lift straighten you out. Practise this posture separately, against a wall if you wish, but continue to feel the lift from your middle.

12 press up Using the shoulder girdle as a hinge, and keeping the arms strong, let yourself drop back into a Press Up. Omit this posture if you are not sure of your ability. Relaxation and stillness must follow this sequence.

Relaxing Sequence

The postures are all designed to get your hips level – or above your head. Inversion takes a great strain from your heart and provides your head with an amount of blood that gravity denies you. With the release of tension from your shoulders and neck, this will leave you feeling lighter.

1 seated forward bend Remember that a forward bend does not automatically require straight legs. Hinge from the hips and lengthen the tummy up and out of the hips.

2 table Take your hands back behind you and, keeping the back open, use your bottom and back to lift you into the Table. Soften the chest to feel the stretch in the chest and the shoulders.

3 cobbler Lower your bottom down and draw the heels towards the crotch. Use your bottom to open the knees towards the floor and hinge forwards through the hips.

7 tortoise Roll up and separate the legs, so that you can hinge through them. Remember, the object is to open the hips and lower spine, not to straighten the legs.

8 shoulder stand Roll down and make the letter "L" with your legs in the air. Pull your knees and shins towards your face to help you engage the abdomen.

9 batfink Roll down to an "L" again and pause momentarily before rolling any residual tension from the back and spine. Take your time and roll as slowly as you can.

4 bridge Roll the spine back on to the floor and continue rolling the hips up into this back bend. Keep the hips long and learn how you can lengthen the lower spine in this pose.

5 double pigeon Come down slowly, choose a leg to cross on top or in front and hinge forwards to open up the hip and lower spine. Change legs.

6 batfink Draw both knees towards the shoulders, while curling the lower spine so you engage the tummy and roll fluently down and up along the spine.

10 fish Having felt your spine open and bow, lie down to remind yourself of the muscles of the upper back. Arch the upper spine by drawing the shoulder blades wide and then down the back.

11 baby Bend your knees to bring the legs up to the chest. Bend the knees so you can push your bottom away from you along the floor. Once again, you feel the hips and lower spine open.

12 corpse Take the heels down to the floor and rest with the knees still up before relaxing fully with the legs down. Give the back plenty of time to adjust to its new length.

Acknowledgements

AUTHOR'S ACKNOWLEDGEMENTS

Judy Smith: I would like to give heartfelt thanks to my guru, Mr Iyengar, who has not only been a wonderfully patient teacher, but who also constantly inspires his students to delve deeper into the art, practice and science of yoga. His knowledge, intuition, intelligence and humour have motivated thousands of yoga practitioners all over the world, and for this we are eternally grateful. I would also like to express my gratitude to Silvia Prescott and Penny Chaplin, my senior teachers, and to my husband, Rob, and my children, Matthew and Cassy, for their continual support and encouragement.

Emily Kelly: Without the help of my associates and dear friends, this book would never have been more than an idea. I would like to thank Michael King and Anoushka for being great teachers; Susan Newsom, Malcolm, Tiffany, Nikki, Saban, Jeanette Haslam, and Alex Fugello; and all my wonderful clients whom I consider to be close friends. I would also like to thank Valerie Foldvary who acted as an advisor on *Pilates*.

Jonathan Monks: Thank you to the space above my mat. Mum and Dad. Julia. Carly. Lesley. Friends, for without you the world seems hard work. Students and all those who continue to show me all that I'm too close to see. The publisher for this opportunity. Play well.

PUBLISHER'S ACKNOWLEDGEMENTS

Iyengar Yoga
Thanks for the loan of props and mats to Paul Walker at Yoga Matters, suppliers of yoga mats, props and clothing. 32 Clarendon Road, London N8 ODJ
tel. 020 8888 8588 fax 020 8888 0623
www.yogamatters.co.uk
for international sales www.yogapropshop.com

Thank you to Stuart Mackay at Beyond Hope for supplying the prana clothing. Contact www.prana.com for stockists.

Pilates
Thanks to the following libraries for supplying images (numbers denote page references):
Gettyone Store: 53R, 119, 120L, 121T, 121B, 122BL, 128 TR
Magnum: 51BL
Superstock Ltd: 120R, 122TR

Yoga-Pilates
Many thanks to Judith Kleinman for allowing us to use the space at Highbury to shoot the photographs; to Sarah Brown for her diligent transcribing; to John Freeman and Alex Dow for creating inspirational images against the light.

Societies and Useful Addresses

Australia
BKS Iyengar Yoga Association of
Australia
PO Box 130, Bayswater WA 6933
www.iyengaryoga.asn.au

The Australian Pilates Method
Association
(for information on Australia-wide
Pilates courses)
www.australianpilates.asn.au

The Body Control Pilates Association
(for information on qualified Pilates
instructors in Australia)
www.bodycontrol.co.uk

Canada
Canadian Iyengar Yoga Teacher's
Association
www.iyengaryogacanada.com

The Body Control Pilates Association
(for information on qualified Pilates
instructors in Canada)
www.bodycontrol.co.uk

India
Ramamani Iyengar Memorial Yoga
Institute (RIMYI)
(the home institute)
Mr Pandurang Rao, Secretary
1107 B/1 Hare Krishna Mandir Road,
Shivaji Nagar, Pune 411 016,
tel. 91 20 565 6134
www.bksiyengar.com

New Zealand
The BKS Iyengar Association of New
Zealand (IYANZ)
PO Box 9278, Wellington
tel. 64 9 571 3110
fax 64 9 571 3101
www.iyengar-yoga.org.nz

Pilates Natural Fitness Studio Ltd
1 Barrys Point Road
Takapuna
Auckland
tel. 64 9 489 1987
email pilatesinstitute@xtra.co.nz
www.pilates.co.nz

South Africa
BKS Iyengar Yoga Institute of
Southern Africa
104 Mowbray Road
Greenside
Gauteng, 2193
tel. 27 11 646 9687
email nmorris@iafrica.com
www.bksiyengar.co.za

For information on Pilates courses
and teacher training in South Africa:
www.pilatessa.com
www.pilatesteachers.co.za

United Kingdom
Iyengar Yoga Institute
223a Randolph Avenue
Maida Vale
London, W9 1NL
tel. 020 7624 3080
www.iyi.org.uk

BKS Iyengar Teacher's Association of
the UK
email info@bksiyta.co.uk
www.bksiyta.co.uk

The Body Control Pilates Association
6 Langley Street
London WC2H 9JA
tel. 020 7379 3734
fax 020 7379 7551
email info@bodycontrol.co.uk
www.bodycontrol.co.uk

Pilates Institute
3rd Floor, Wimborne House
151–155 New North Road
London W1 6TA
tel. 020 7253 3177
www.pilates-institute.com

Danceworks (Jonathan Monks)
16 Balderton Street
London W1K 6TN
tel. 020 7629 6183
email info@danceworks.co.uk
www.danceworks.co.uk

United States
For listings of yoga institutes in
Canada and the US:
www.yogadirectory.com
www.jivamuktiyoga.com

BKS Iyengar Yoga National
Assocation of the United States
1676 Hilton Head Ct., #2288
El Cajon, CA 92019
tel. 800 889 9642
www.iynaus.org

Balanced Body (Pilates)
8200 Ferguson Avenue
Sacramento, CA 95828
tel. 916 388 2838
www.pilates.com

Index

index